Dialogue and
Discovery

SUNY Series in Philosophy
Robert C. Neville, Editor

Dialogue and Discovery

A Study in Socratic Method

Kenneth Seeskin

State University of New York Press • Albany

183.2
Se36d

TO BRONNA

Published by
State University of New York Press, Albany

© 1987   State University of New York

All rights reserved

Printed in the United States of America

No part of this book may be used or reproduced
in any manner whatsoever without written permission
except in the case of brief quotations embodied in
critical articles and reviews.

For information, address State University of New York
Press, State University Plaza, Albany, N.Y., 12246

Library of Congress Cataloging in Publication Data

Seeskin, Kenneth, 1947-
    Dialogue and discovery.

    (SUNY series in philosophy)
    Bibliography: p.
    1. Socrates—Contributions in methodology.
2. Methodology—History. I. Title.   II. Series.
B318.M48S43   1986   183'.2   86-14514
ISBN 0-88706-337-3
ISBN 0-88706-336-5 (pbk.)

10 9 8 7 6 5 4 3 2 1

Contents

Preface

WHY ANOTHER BOOK on Socrates?
The answer is not that the existing literature is grossly inadequate. A number of good histories, philosophical studies, and line by line commentaries are already available. There are, I think, two reasons why this book is needed at the present time.

The first has to do with my perception of the current philosophical climate. I think it fair to say that philosophers are not as confident as they were five or six decades ago. Claims of certainty, comprehensive understanding, and privileged access are still being made but not with the same frequency. Today the mood is often one of qualification or retreat. If this assessment is correct, it is important that we consider the thought of a philosopher who openly admitted he had not achieved the knowledge he was looking for and expressed doubts that any living person would. He was not a skeptic as that term is usually employed, but his willingness to admit failure is something of a rarity in the history of philosophy and deserves consideration.

The second has to do with the current state of scholarship on the Socratic dialogues. A person who had never read a dialogue but was presented with much of the secondary literature written on them would never guess, in fact would be shocked to hear, that the original text is a drama. For many commentators, the only challenge is to identify the fewest number of premises from which the conclusions of Socratic philosophy can be deduced. This is all that is meant by *interpretation*. On the other hand, there is also secondary literature from which one could never guess that the drama had important philosophical consequences. In this case, *interpretation* means setting the scene, identifying literary allusions, and speculating on the order of the dialogues.

The present study attempts to avoid both extremes. It is my purpose to show that the subject matter of Socratic philosophy, virtue, its method, refutation, and its form, dialogue, are all related. They are all related by virtue of being directed to one end: the moral improvement of the respondent. So in addition to identifying the premises of Socrates' arguments and the scene in which the discussion takes place, we have to ask ourselves how the respondents actually behave.

There are a number of people who deserve special thanks for the preparation of this book. First and foremost is Robert Brumbaugh for good advice, helpful suggestions, and a lot of patience. My colleague Martin Mueller should be thanked for assistance in the translation of Gorgias' *Apology of Palamedes*. Four anonymous readers are to be thanked for what were, on the whole, excellent criticisms. A number of people have helped in an indirect way through comments, papers, and discussions over the years; they include: Richard Kraut, Reginald Allen, Michael Morgan, Joseph Edelheit, and John McCumber. Finally it should be said that substantial portions of the first and third chapter have appeared in *Philosophy and Literature*. I wish to thank the Journal, its publisher, the Johns Hopkins University Press, and its gifted editor, Denis Dutton, for permission to use this material in the present study.

All translations of Greek texts are my own unless otherwise indicated.

Chapter One
Socratic Philosophy and the Dialogue Form

P HILOSOPHY DOES NOT BECOME literature merely because it is written in dialogue form. We could take the latest issue of the *Journal of Philosophy*, invent dummy characters, think of leading questions, and come up with a "dialogue" which would have no literary significance whatever. Even if it were written by a gifted stylist, it would not become literature unless the dialogue form were an integral part of the author's conception of philosophy. To put this in a different way, not all philosophy can become literature. In most cases, a philosopher's ability to write well is a bonus: it makes him easier to read and teach but does not affect the direction of the argument.[1] Hume was an accomplished writer, but there is no reason to regard the *Treatise* as a work of literature. Its conclusions would not be altered even if they had been written in the rumble-bumble prose of Kant. It is only when form and content work together that a piece of philosophy can claim literary significance.

1. DIALOGUE AS A MORAL TEST

One case where they do work together is the Socratic dialogue.[2] It is clear that a great deal would be lost if Socratic philosophy were written in straight, expository prose. As Gregory Vlastos once noted, Socrates does not just have conclusions to impart but a method for arriving at them.[3] That method is *elenchus*, which means to examine, refute, or put to shame. As practised by Socrates, it is a method which lends itself to the dialogue because it requires that at least two voices be heard. It requires, in addition, that the people whose voices we hear be intimately connected with the positions they take. The first rule of Socratic *elenchus* is that the respondent must say what he really thinks. When Protagoras attempts to break this rule by adopt-

ing a hypothetical view about the nature of virtue (331c), Socrates
stops him immediately:

> PROT: I don't think it is quite so simple, Socrates, so that I
>   should grant that justice is holy and holiness just. It
>   seems to me there is a distinction here. But what dif-
>   ference does it make? If you wish, let us agree that
>   justice is holy and holiness just.
>
> SOC: Oh, no! I don't want to examine this "If you like" or
>   "If you think" but to examine you and me. When I
>   say "you and me" I mean that one can best examine
>   the issue by taking away the "ifs".

In the *Gorgias*, when Callicles shows hesitation in answering Socrates,
Socrates replies that unless Callicles has the courage to speak freely, the
inquiry cannot proceed (494c ff.). Even when the respondent's com-
pliance would make his job much easier, Socrates insists that the respondent not say anything short of what he truly believes (e.g., *Crito* 49d).

The result is that the respondent has more at stake than the out-
come of a philosophical argument: to the degree that he follows
Socrates' rule, he is putting his life on the line. As Nicias tells
Lysimachus in the *Laches* (187e–188a):

> . . . whoever comes into contact with Socrates and talks with
> him face to face, is certain to be drawn into a discussion with
> him. And no matter where the discussion begins, he is carried
> round and cannot stop until he is led to give an account of
> himself, and of the manner in which he now lives his life and
> the kind of life he has lived up to that point. And once he has
> been led to do that, Socrates will not let him go until he has
> thoroughly and properly put all his ways to the test.

It is impossible in a Socratic context to defend a position at odds with
one's own behavior. At stake are the moral intuitions which underlie
everything one stands for. Protagoras has a great deal to lose if it
should turn out that virtue is not teachable, Gorgias if it should turn
out that rhetoric is not an art, Euthyphro if it should turn out that prosecuting one's father for murder is impious, Laches if it should turn
out that courage requires knowledge not normally at the disposal of a
battlefield general.

We may therefore agree with Dorothy Tarrant that there is more in
a Socratic dialogue than the author's love of drama:[4]

> The essence of dialogue lies in the interaction of human
> minds. For Plato the human individual—whether as perci-

pient, as moral agent, or as spiritual being—stands in the centre and forefront of his thought. Here he is obviously following Socrates, but he develops the theme in his own ways, and he seldom strays far from it. Because this is his central interest, it becomes natural to express all his thought in the form of personal utterance by one individual or another (not necessarily or always by the Socrates who is normally the chief speaker), and to work out its development in terms of progressive agreement between such individuals.

Tarrant's point cannot be emphasized strongly enough. What is at stake in a Socratic dialogue is not, at least not primarily, the logical relations between propositions but the interaction of moral agents. That is what Socrates means when he refuses to allow Protagoras to use hypotheticals and claims that what he really wants to examine are ''you and me.''

It follows that *elenchus* is more than an exercise in philosophical analysis. In asking people to state and defend the moral intuitions which underlie their way of life, Socrates inevitably reveals something about their characters. *Elenchus,* then, has as much to do with honesty, reasonableness, and courage as it does with logical acumen: the honesty to say what one really thinks, the reasonableness to admit what one does not know, and the courage to continue the investigation. Most of Socrates' respondents are lacking in all three. Protagoras becomes angry, Polus resorts to cheap rhetorical tricks, Callicles begins to sulk, Critias loses his self-control, Meno wants to quit. While their reactions leave much to be desired, Socrates' respondents do emerge from the pages of the dialogues as real people. Not only is three a clash of ideas but a clash of the personalities who have adopted them. So while the Socratic dialogues deal with virtue, they are never simple morality plays.

This book argues that *elenchus* is central to Socratic philosophy and that only if we understand how *elenchus* places moral demands on questioner and respondent will that philosophy make sense. The purpose of *elenchus* is to facilitate discovery, but in a Socratic context, discovey is not a sudden flash of illumination; it is something which must be prepared for, something which the soul must earn. The subject of Socratic epistemology, then, is, in Tarrant's words, a moral agent. To acquire knowledge, the soul must free itself of the anger, arrogance, and laziness present in so many of Socrates' companions. The importance of ethics to epistemology is all the more obvious if we conceive of the search for knowledge in dialogical terms. If nothing else, dialogue requires cooperation with another person, which, in turn, requires appropriate forms of behavior. This entire way of looking at knowledge comes to a head in the Socratic dictum that virtue is knowledge. Unless we understand how knowledge comes to be present, this claim, the heart of Socratic philosophy, is likely to seem absurd.

2. DIALOGUE AND THE WRITTEN WORD

It is noteworthy that despite his literary gifts, Plato was suspicious of writing philosophy. In the *Phaedrus* (275d-e), he has Socrates say according to Hackforth's translation:[5]

> You know, Phaedrus, that's the strange thing about writing, which makes it truly analogous to painting. The painter's products stand before us as though they were alive; but if you question them, they maintain a most majestic silence. It is the same with written words: they seem to talk to you as though they were intelligent, but if you ask them anything about what they say, from a desire to be instructed, they go on telling you just the same thing for ever. And once a thing is put in writing, the composition, whatever it may be, drifts all over the place, getting into the hands not only of those who understand it, but equally of those who have no business with it; it doesn't know how to address the right people, and not address the wrong. And when it is ill-treated and unfairly abused it always needs its parent to come to its help, being unable to defend or help itself.

An analogous sentiment is expressed in the *Seventh Epistle* (341–4) and suggests that Plato regarded the dialogue form as a philosophical *deuteros plous*, a second best. Though it cannot take the place of actual conversation, it is a better medium in which to represent such conversation than is prose. I say *represent* because Socrates goes on to claim in this passage that the written word is an image (*eidōlon*, 276a) of the spoken one.[6] Still, it is possible for one image to be more faithful than another. The writer of a treatise is, in effect, delivering a long speech to the reader. Socrates' dislike of long speeches was notorious and is justified by reasons similar to those which led Plato to distrust the written word: the listener cannot question the speaker and is forced to become a passive participant.

In a dialogue, the author is not delivering a long speech but directing a conversation. If his direction is successful, if he has mastered the art of dialogue in the way Plato did, the reader is no longer feels that she is in a passive role. According to Paul Friedländer:[7]

> For the written dialogue transmits its dialogical and dialectical dynamics to the reader. To him is addressed every question raised by Socrates; every aye of Glaukon or Lysis is his aye— or his nay—and this dialogical dynamics continues to echo within him beyone the conclusion. The dialogue is the only form of book that seems to suspend the book form itself.

The word *seems* is important. Nothing can take the place of actually submitting to the rigors of *elenchus*. But if we have to settle for a second best, the dialogue is superior to the treatise.

Yet there is more to the choice of dialogue than this. It is a cornerstone of Socratic epistemology that what people normally call *teaching* is impossible.[8] That is, it is impossible to impart true propositions to another person and expect that person to come away with knowledge. It follows not only that Socrates cannot teach the respondent (*Apology* 33a), but that Plato, the author trying to preserve his memory, cannot teach the reader. It is not that the reader or the respondent is ignorant of something which Socrates and Plato are convinced they know. Rather it is that the reader or the respondent already has the knowledge he is looking for but is having trouble getting hold of it. As Laches says to Socrates after failing to define courage (194b):

> I am truly angry with myself and am not able to say what I have in mind. It seems to me that I know what courage is, but somehow is has escaped me so that I cannot put into words exactly what it is.

It is true that Socratic philosophy involves *elenchus* or refutation; but we will miss an important point if we do not see that in this context, refutation is not purely destructive. It is destructive in order to be therapeutic (*Sophist* 230b-d)—like the doctor who must cut and burn in order to heal. In the last analysis, the purpose of such refutation is to enable the respondent to say what he feels he was trying to say all along.

Socrates never claims that *elenchus* can work miracles. In the *Republic* (518b-d), he is critical of those who think they can put sight in blind eyes. What it can do is "point the soul in the right direction" by helping someone who has a partial grasp of reality become clearer about what he thinks he sees. To assume that the respondent comes to the discussion already in some sense aware of what he is trying to learn is to assume a particular theory of the human mind: that the contents of the mind extend beyond the fairly limited scope of immediate awareness. Thus Socrates claims in the *Meno* (85c) that the slave's opinions about geometry are somehow "in" his soul even though he has never had a lesson in the subject. The reason is that the slave's opinions are really his and that Socrates did not put them there: all Socrates did was ask questions. From a modern perspective, the claim that the slave's opinions are "in" the soul raises more questions than it answers. Does it commit Socrates to a theory of innate ideas or only to a theory of innate capacities? Is there a criterion to decide which ideas are "in" the soul and is this criterion anything more than our notion of *a priori* truth? What is the relation between the idea "in" the soul and the reality it depicts or represents? Some of these questions will be discussed in a later chapter. For the present, all we need to agree on is this: it is possible for a person to have opinions she has not considered or is not fully aware of. She has the opinions in the sense that she feels confident that a question should be answered in a particular way, but the question may never have been put to her before. Or, she can have opinions she is fully aware of but consequences she is not. That is why Socrates can tell Polus at *Gorgias* 474b that he does not really believe what he is saying. Obviously Polus is committed to what he is saying. The point is that unbeknownst to him, his views are incompatible with premises he and everyone else are predisposed to accept.

Once we admit that a person may have opinions she has not considered or may not really believe what she is saying, we allow for the possibility that the determination of what one *does* believe can constitute a genuine discovery. It is in this sense that Socrates can say that the ideas present in the soul may require considerable effort, even courage, to retrieve (*Meno* 81d). With the possible exception of Meno's slave, no one in the early dialogues is courageous enough. Euthyphro walks away, Meno leaves town, Critias and Alcibiades go on to other things. The irony is that they are running away from the discovery of what they themselves really think.

Notice, however, that on this view of philosophy, there is an additional reason for objecting to straight, expository prose. Prose, after all, is a teaching device in the sense in which Socrates was opposed to teaching; its purpose is to fill the reader in rather than draw her out. If we ask what would be needed to draw the reader out, the answer is perhaps more psychological than logical: whatever it takes to get her to discard her old ways of thinking and approach the problem from a new perspective. The assumption at work here is that the purpose of a Socratic dialogue is, as Jacob Klein put it, to continue Socrates' work.[9] As Klein points out, such a view is hardly novel; it derives from Schleiermacher. It is no surprise, then, that the dialogues contain a number of devices whose purpose is to foster the conceptual break-through which Socrates wants the respondent to achieve and which, in turn, Plato wants the reader to achieve: irony flattery, satire, paradox, myth, mockery—all the things which make the dialogues so delightful to read. It is important to understand, however, that these devices are not employed for their literary value alone. If it is a mistake to ignore the literary side of the dialogues and concentrate on the underlying "doctrine", it is equally a mistake to treat the literary side as pure art and thus, to use Klein's expression, render it autonomous.[10] The literary devices are part of the *elenchus* and have a definite epistemological function: they are spurs to inquiry and therefore to discovery.

On the other hand, the Socratic understanding of philosophy gives to literature a greater significance than other philosophers would allow or than Socrates himself allows in passages where the issue of literature is brought up. If we assume that the reader is not a blank tablet but comes to the text with the latent knowledge required by the theory of recollection, why should literature not be as good as anything else in bringing ideas to a conscious level? Indeed, why should it not be far better than expository prose for just the reason Socrates gave: expository prose puts the reader in a passive position. Literature, on the other hand, engages her, arouses her, shocks or amuses her and therefore is better suited to the goals of Socratic philosophy. What I have in mind here is a theory of interpretation which takes as its model not *mimēsis*, which is the central notion in Klein's interpretation, but *anamnēsis*; not imitation but recollection. True, there are mimetic features in many Socratic dialogues. But they would serve no purpose unless we assume that, as the respondent comes to the discussion already aware of what he is trying to learn, so the reader comes to the text. The reason Plato has the characters imitate certain actions or exemplify the form of behavior they are trying to understand is that such characteristizations strike a responsive chord in the reader, i.e., they assist the reader in "recalling" the knowledge she has but cannot quite get hold of.

3. HIDING BEHIND THE WRITTEN WORD

To pursue the idea that the text is meant to assist in the process of recollection, we must rule out a tempting but textually unfounded suggestion. It is often argued that the reason Plato chose the dialogue form is that he had no system or doctrine. According to John Herman Randall: "Plato . . . knew too much about life to put it into a system."[11] On this view, the purpose of the dialogues is to present us with a variey of philosophical alternatives and allow us to watch as they play off against one another. The dialogues depict philosophical inquiry in all its stages and forms; they are, as one commentator put it, slices of the philosophical life.[12] Notice how this interpretation puts both the author and the reader in a peculiar role. The author, Plato, is not really saying anything, he is only exhibiting the things other people say. He possesses what Keats termed *negative capability* in the sense that no position taken in the course of a discussion can be attributed to the author.[13] The reader is put in a position to observe a philosophical exchange but is not expected to come away from it with any particular feeling or attitude.

Without raising the time-honored question of which ideas belong to the historical Socrates and which to Plato, a question which centuries of debate have done nothing to resolve, we can say that *Plato* was asserting something when he had Socrates defend a particular conception of human life. And if we look at how Socrates is actually portrayed, we find that the was not someone who engaged in philosophical inquiry merely for its own sake. According to his account of the philosophical enterprise; he was engaged in a form of persuasion (*Apology* 30a, 36c). The dialogues present him as a man with deep moral convictions and as someone who strove to get others to share them. As Gregory Vlastos put it: "no man ever breathed greater assurance that his feet were planted firmly on the path of right."[14] That is why Socrates can tell so formidable an opponent as Callicles that as long as he resists Socrates' conclusions about virtue, he will contradict himself (*Gorgias* 482b); in other words, there is no reasonable alternative to his view, or at least none that Callicles would be willing to accept. No doubt Socrates was willing to follow the best argument wherever it takes him (*Crito* 46b), but this did not prevent him from having strong feelings about where that might be. When he tells Polus that the truth can never be refuted (*Gorgias* 473b), he does so in the context of his conviction that it is better to suffer injustice than to commit it. What he is saying is that any argument which appears to overturn this conclusion must be spurious. So it is wrong to think that Socrates was interested only in pointing out the inconsistencies in other people's opinions.[15] In the *Crito* and *Gorgias*, he points out inconsistencies in order to persuade the respondent of the truth of his own contention. In the *Apology*, he says several times that the purpose of the *elenchus* is to get people to pay more attention to the welfare of their souls. In the dialogues of search, it is to free people from what he regards as the evils of popular opinion.

To say that Socrates had deep convictions on how to live a life is not to say that he had knowledge.[16] By his own admission, knowledge requires more than a conviction that one's opinions are true. It requires that one can define the key terms of moral discourse and show how his beliefs are necessitated by those definitions. This Socrates never claimed he could do. We will see in a later chapter that the knowledge he claimed to have is *human* knowledge, which means that it is by nature imperfect. All of this is compatible with saying that Socrates was as much in the business of saving souls as any radio dial preacher. He clearly believed that he was sent to awaken the city of Athens from its dogmatic slumbers. His methods might differ from those of a radio dial preacher, but he was just as serious about what he was doing and just as exhuberant in his pitch. In the *Apology* (30b), he claims that from virtue as he conceives it comes money and "all other human goods, both public and private." So convinced was he of the truth of this message that he abandoned everything else in life to propagate it.

On the other hand, there can be little doubt that Socrates is not just a character in Plato's dialogues but a hero of extraordinary proportions. At the end of the *Meno*, he suggests that Socrates was among the living what Teiresias was among the dead: "He alone kept his wits, the rest darted about like shadows." To write these words about someone in the business of saving souls is to enter that business oneself. It follows that Plato was interested in more than slices of the philosophical life. Or, to put it another way, he was interested in slices of the philosophical life only to the extent that they made the reader turn to and reflect on the moral truths which Socrates espoused. With certain qualifications we can say that Plato, too, wished to assert that care of the soul ought to be the chief concern of one's life, that it is better to suffer injustice than to commit it, etc. The reason he wrote dialogues was not to hide behind a veil of anonymity but to avoid having to teach what the soul must discover for itself.

4. EPISTEMOLOGICAL OPTIMISM

It will be objected that is socrates was so committed to saving souls, the appropriate form in which to preserve his memory is not dialogue but something like homily. Instead of having him pull someone aside and inquire about virtue, Plato should have him mount the pulpit and exhort people to live better lives. That there is real force to this objection is seen by the fact that there are passages where he does just this: the end of the *Gorgias* is an obvious example. The objection points out the problem Plato faced as a dramatic artist. Because he was suspicious of the written word, he could not put his thoughts on paper in an unreflective way. He had to take seriously the relation of the reader to the text. If the reader came to approach the text as a student approaches a teacher, then from Plato's perspective, the text would fail. These considerations led him to chose the dialogue over the treatise. But if the purpose of the dialogue is to assist the soul in recovering moral truths, he ran the risk of turning the dialogues into sermons in which Socrates gets the interesting lines and all the respondents say is "Amen." A sermon is not a true dialogue; on the other hand a true dialogue might leave the reader confused on what the point of the conversation was. What makes the Socratic dialogues lasting works of art is the way Plato overcame this difficulty. In Plato's hands the dialogue form is more than a convenient way of refuting opponents, it is a form in which the characters enjoy a remarkable degree of autonomy. Whatever else they might be, Callicles, Thrasymachus, and Alcibiades are not straw men. Although they may not win their respective arguments, they state them as persuasively as anyone has and leave a lasting impression on the reader.

On the other hand, Socrates does not win either, or at least not always. We know that he was committed to the unity of virtue and knowledge, but for all its attractiveness, this thesis never appears as a dialectical panacea. It is raised explicitly in the *Laches*, *Meno*, and *Protagoras*; but in no case is it the final conclusion of an argument. As Myles Burnyeat put it: "The idea of virtue as knowledge is indeed less a conclusion at which discussion can rest than a starting-point for a new approach—a better one to be sure, but not without difficulties of its own to be cleared up before its philosophical benefits can be finally confirmed.''[17] Thus the *Meno* and *Protagoras* each end by saying that the search for a definition must now *begin*. It is safe to say, then, that while Socrates normally gets the best of his opponent, his victories are partial. He never emerges from a conversation in the triumphant way that Augustine emerges from some of his dialogues or Philonous emerges from Berkeley's. Take the *Protagoras*. After a series of preliminary skirmishes, the great sophist stakes his reputation on a distinction between courage and knowledge. While Socrates manages to convince him that they are the same, the dialogue never suggests that Socrates is wholly right. Knowledge is teachable. Therefore if courage is knowledge, it is teachable. But at the beginning of the dialogue, Socrates had arued, against Protagoras, that virtue is *not* teachable. So it seems that the two major characters have switched positions. Who, then, is the victor? Plato does not tell us.

It could still be objected that if his silence overcomes the tendency to preach, it creates an equally serious problem: the tendency to confuse. To the extent that a Socratic dialogue produces confusion, it runs the risk that like so many of Socrates' respondents, the reader will grow weary and want to quit. Consider the case of Hume's *Dialogues Concerning Natural Religion*. Here the three main characters all succeed in destroying one another's arguments. There are some beautifully written speeches and some *Protagoras*-like reversals. Yet the readers is not left with the impression that inquiry on theological questions ought to continue. She begins to suspect, as Hume no doubt wanted her to, that the paradoxes encountered in the course of the discussion are unavoidable. That is, she begins to be suspect that there is something wrong with the subject matter so that further inquiry along these lines is a waste of time.

No such impression is created by the Socratic dialogues. On the contrary, the reader is led to believe that, like Meno's slave, she is on the verge of a great discovery—that he has only to fiddle with the premises of the argument to see what Plato is trying to say. Again the response of Laches: "It seems to me that I know what courage is, but somehow it has escaped me so that I cannot put into words exactly what it is." That is how the reader feels, too, and is why she comes away from the text with a surge of optimism. The answer is staring her in the face. If she does not see it at first, it must be that she has a mental block. As Grote put it: "Interpreters sift with microscopic accuracy the negative dialogues of Plato, in hopes of detecting the ultimate elements of that positive solution which he is supposed to have lodged therein, and which, when found, may be put together so as to clear up all the antecedent difficulties.''[18] So the reader does not come away thinking there is something wrong with the subject matter. Once the fog clears, all the pieces will fit together like a puzzle.

That this impression is false is attested to by centuries of Platonic scholarship and by the fact that Socrates never claimed to have cleared up all the ''antecedent difficulties.'' But the illusory quality of the impression does not belittle Plato's ability as an artist. He has managed to convince the reader that the obstacles which stand in the way of a solution are temporary. The classic expression of optimism is found in the *Meno* (81c–d):[19]

> Therefore since the soul is immortal and has been born many times, and has seen all things in this world and the next, there is nothing it has not learned. So it should not surprise us that it can recollect what it knew before—concerning virtue and other things as well. Since all nature is akin, and the soul has learned all things, there is nothing to prevent someone, having recalled only one thing—what we call *learning*—from discovering all the rest, if he is brave and does not grow tired of inquiring.

We have only to pull ourselves together and continue the search to unlock the mysteries of the universe.

It is easy for the reader to get swept away by this optimism and to lose sight of her own limitations. This point was not lost on Nietzsche, who said in *The Birth of Tragedy*: ''Anyone who has ever experienced the pleasure of Socratic insight and felt how, spreading in ever-widening circles, it seeks to embrace the whole world of appearances, will never again find any stimulus toward existence more violent than the craving to complete this conquest and to weave the net impenetrably tight.''[20] The result is what Nietzsche terms ''Greek cheerfulness.'' Whether cheerfulness is all that the Socratic dialogues convey will be discussed below. For the present it is worth noting how the dialogues are structured so as to constantly reassure the reader that she is making progress.

It is very rare that a Socratic dialogue is a haphazard discussion or a simple deductive exercise. In most cases there is a pattern to the various twists and turns. We have seen that in the *Protagoras*, it is a criss-cross. Socrates thinks virtue is not teachable, Protagoras that it is; but in the end they appear to be on opposite sides of the issue. In the *Laches* and *Charmides*, it is a Scylla and Charybdis. A particular virtue is at issue. One of the characters (e.g., Critias) is too brash while the other (e.g., Charmides) is too shy.[21] In the *Symposium*, it is an ascending hierarchy. Each speaker raises the level of discussion and prepares the way for the speech of Socrates. These structures do more than satisfy the reader's desire for tidyness, they make her think that she is being carried along by a logical current which will deposit her in exactly the right place. In the *Symposium* she becomes so caught up in the flow of the argument that she almost forgets it *is* an argument. The epistemological effect is equally pronounced: the reader comes to feel that she knows what is going to happen next. It is like listening to a symphony and being asked to predict the last five notes. The difference is that in a Socratic dialogue, we never find out what the last five notes are. The structures which Plato works so hard to establish point us in the right direction but never quite give the problem away. The result is, as Kierkegaard once noted, that if we do make a discovery after reading a Socratic dialogue, the credit does not go to Socrates but to us.[22] Socrates, it will be remembered, is not a teacher because teaching is impossible.

It is no accident, then, that in the *Theaetetus* Plato has Socrates compare himself to a midwife. It is the respondent, and by implication the reader, who gives birth to an idea. All Socrates does is facilitate the delivery. In this way, the reader is given every possible motive to inquire. She is taken to the doorstep of a solution and told that if she crosses the threshold, she is the one who will receive praise.

5. IMPENDING TRAGEDY

If such optimism went unchecked, the Socratic dialogues might qualify as works of literature, but they would still leave a lot to be desired. Socrates lived through a long and bitterly contested war which culminated in the collapse of the Athenian empire. Although Socrates served the city in combat, he was eventually put to death by the people most in need of his message. Plato had no choice but to balance Socrates' optimism with a sense of impending tragedy. The *Euthyphro* and *Meno* contain obvious references to his trial for impiety. In the *Gorgias*, Callicles tells him point blank that if he is brought to trial on trumped up charged, he will have nothing to say in his own defense (486a ff.). The *Symposium*, often regarded as Plato's great comedy, is narrated by a man who cannot control his weeping in the *Phaedo*. But these references have been discussed many times. I believe the real sense of impending tragedy is psychological—that for all of his efforts, Socrates never does persuade anyone to alter his life. His closest associates, Critias and Alcibiades, became a disgrace to the city. Meno went on to a life of treachery in Asia Minor and was executed. Laches and Nicias both met with misfortune. Neither Gorgias nor Protagoras was moved to abandon sophistry and pursue philosophy. Worst of all, his longtime companion Crito accused him of cowardice for not breaking the law (*Crito* 45c ff.)—thereby proving that he missed the whole point of Socrates' speech to the jury. Callicles sums up the feeling of most respondents when, after hearing Socrates discourse on how to live a life, he says (*Gorgias* 513c): "I don't know why but somehow what you say strikes me as right, Socrates, and yet I feel as most people do: you don't quite convince me."[23]

Nor, as far as I can determine, does he convince the reader. We are anxious to follow Socrates through the pages of the dialogue and equally anxious to go on talking about virtue after putting the dialogue down. But do we really think our lives will be transformed? We know that we will not, and if my interpretation is right, Plato knew it too. There is a profound truth in Alcibiades' claim that the one overriding emotion Socrates produces is shame (*Symposium* 216b): "I cannot disavow the duty to do what he bids me to do, but as soon as I am out of his presence, I fall victim to the worship of the crowd. So I run away from him, and when I see him again, become ashamed of my former admissions." We have seen that by definition shame is an essential part of the elenctic process. In the *Apology* (29d-e), Socrates summarizes his mission in the following way:

> My good man, you are a citizen of Athens, the greatest city in the world and most famous for wisdom and power, are you not ashamed for paying more attention to wealth, reputation, and honor than to wisdom, truth, and the perfection of your soul?

He is equally explicit in the *Sophist* (230c-d), where he claims that the soul will receive no benefit from the application of knowledge until it is refuted and brought to shame.

Socrates showed that when it came to virtue, the great thinkers of his day knew next to nothing. We watch with great relish as he brings

Gorgias and Protagoras to their knees. But it is impossible to read these dialogues without thinking that *our* claim to knowledge would fair no better. The Socratic dictum that compared to the knowledge a god might possess, human knowledge is of little or no value (*Apology* 23a–b), is not restricted to fifth century Athens. It is offered as a general comment about the human condition. So if Gorgias, Protagoras, and the others pull themselves together and go on pretending to be wise, it is likely that we will too. Like Alcibiades, we may feel shame when confronted with our former admission and think about running away, but neither emotion will prevent us from repeating the story over again.

The emotional reaction most closely associated with the tragic hero is not shame but pity and fear. With Oedipus, we have someone as committed to inquiry as Socrates was. In the context of Sophocles' play, however, the audience knows what the major character does not: that the inquiry, if successful, will lead to a catastrophic result. The tragedy of the situation is that divine omniscience has to assert itself but can do so only at the cost of human suffering. The result is pity for the person who must bear the brunt of that suffering and fear to the extent that our situation resembles his. As Bernard Knox put it: " . . . even the most profoundly religious spectator must recoil in horror from the catastrophe to which Oedipus so energetically forces his way."[24]

Socrates' tragedy is quite different. In the first place, there is no catastrophe waiting for him at the end of the intellectual process. Rather than the victim of divine omniscience, the Socrates of the *Apology* describes himself as its servant (23b–c).[25] In pursuing philosophy, he is carrying out the wishes of god. As for the prospect of his own death, he is convinced that no evil can befall a good man either in this life or the next (*Apology* 41c–d). Instead of recoiling at the prospect of his death, Socrates approaches it with equanimity. According to Nietzsche: "He went to his death with the calm with which, according to Plato's description, he leaves the Symposium at dawn."[26] Where then, is there an occasion for pity and fear?

The answer is that there is not insofar as Socrates, the tragic hero, is concerned. Phaedo, the one who reports on the death scene, claims that he was filled with a strange emotion (*Phaedo* 58e). Instead of feeling pity, as he naturally would at the death of a friend, he felt an unusual mixture of pleasure and pain. At the end of the dialogue, Phaedo, like others begins to weep—not for Socrates but for himself. The reader will recall that in the *Apology* (30c), Socrates maintained that his death would not injure him as much as it would the citizens of Athens. In any case, Socrates scolds those who begin to weep at the end of the *Phaedo,* and in characteristic fashion, they feel ashamed of themselves (*Phaedo* 117e).

The dramatic impact of Socrates death is exactly the one he had in life: an unusual mixture of pleasure and pain. It is impossible for the reader not to be aroused by the optimism generated by the inquisitive process but simultaneously to be dismayed by the realization that like so many others, she will resist the conclusions to which it leads her. We saw before that the knowledge already present in the soul requires courage to recover. To the extent that we do not recover it, we, too, are made to feel shame. In this way, the image of the dying Socrates produces in the audience a sense of unworthiness. We stand in awe of Socrates, but for that very reason, we know that our own actions will never compare to his. We are not going to put aside our careers, detach ourselves from all unsupported beliefs, and follow what Nietzsche and Vlastos jointly describe as Socrates' "despotic logic."

Nietzsche objected that in Socrates' optimism lies the death of tragedy.[27] We can now see why this judgment is unfair. It would be more accurate to say that in his portrayal of Socrates, Plato has created a new kind of tragedy. Instead of the hero bearing the brunt of the suffering and allowing the audience to think "There but for the grace of God go I," Plato reverses things. It is the audience who suffer when the dying hero forces them to examine their lives. Despite everything Socrates has said about the immortality of the soul, the audience, too, is inclined to weep and to be scolded. Unlike Oedipus and the other classical heroes, Socrates does not give the audience the luxury of vicarious emotions. As Phaedo rightly points out, we weep for ourselves. The effect of Plato's reversal is thus clear: in a real sense, the tragedy is ours.

6. THE FUSION OF TRAGEDY AND COMEDY

It was argued above that what makes the Socratic dialogues lasting works of art is the way Plato overcame the desire to preach. He did this by affecting a subtle interplay between opposite tendencies or emotions. We are given enough confidence to think that a solution to the problem at hand is immanent but not so much confidence that we lose sight of our own limitations in trying to solve it. At the end of the *Symposium*, there is a famous passage in which Socrates suggests that tragedy and comedy might be two sides of the same thing. From the context it is not clear whether Plato intended this remark to apply to his own work. But intended or not, the comparison is obvious. It is no accident that Phaedo finds himself both laughing and crying at the death of Socrates. Socratic philosophy combines what Nietzsche termed "Greek cheerfulness" with what several characters, including Socrates, refer to as a sense of shame.

Friedländer maintained that the greatest testament to Plato's artistic genius is that we take what he created as historical reality.[28] So successful was Plato in overcoming the desire to preach that the dialogues read like actual conversations. But actual conversations are not necessarily worth repeating. It is not only their liveliness which makes the Socratic dialogues unsurpassed works of art, or the care with which Plato sets the scene, or the many literary and historical illusions they contain. These things are important but not sufficient for the production of a work of genius. What makes them unsurpassed works of art is the way in which they stimulate inquiry and with it, self-examination. It is, in short, the fact that the Socratic dialogues assist in the process of recollection which makes them succeed both as art and as philosphy. Let us recall Socrates' remark about putting sight in blind eyes. If a simple morality play makes for dull reading, it is also a poor way in which to lead a person to an insight. It is a truth of aesthetics as much as epistemology that the only insights worth having are those we can somehow call our own. The greatness of the Socratic dialogues is the way in which truth and beauty, form and substance, are ultimately united.

The purpose of this chapter has been to set forth the principles of Socratic philosophy in a general way and show how they make dialogue the proper vehicle for its expression. But it will not do for a discussion of Socratic philosophy to remain at such a level of generality. The real test of whether truth and beauty, form and substance, work together must lead to the analysis of specific texts. In what follows, I will examine a number of dialogues, chiefly the *Apology*, *Gorgias*, and *Meno*, to prove my point. All of this will help us to understand how the elenctic method, knowledge, and virtue are related. With this understanding in hand, we will be in a position to discuss the Socratic identification of virtue with knowledge.

Notes to Chapter One

1. On this point, see the introduction to Bryan Magee's interview with Iris Murdoch in Magee, *Men of Ideas* (New York: Viking Press, 1978), 264. It is unfortunate that neither Magee nor so gifted a writer as Iris Murdoch ever consider the possibility that the literary qualities of a work may be essential to its success as a piece of philosophy.

2. For the purpose of this discussion, the term "Socratic dialogue" will refer primarily to the dialogues of Plato's early period. This does not mean, however, that supporting evidence from later dialogues will be excluded if it bears on an important point. The best overall discussion of the literary significance of the Socratic dialogues is Paul Friedländer, *Plato: The Dialogues . . . First Period*, translated by H. Meyerhoff (New York, Bollingen, 1964). Other sources include: Julius Stenzel, "The Literary Form and Philosophical content of the Platonic Dialogue," in *Plato's Method of Dialectic*, translated by D. J. Allan (Oxford: Clarendon Press, 1940), 1–22, Philip Merlan, "Form and Content in Plato's Philosophy," *Journal of the History of Ideas* 8 (1947), 406–30, Dorothy Tarrant, "Style and Thought in Plato Dialogues," *Classical Quarterly* 42 (1948), 28–34, Jacob Klein, *A Commentary on Plato's Meno* (Chapel Hill: University of North Carolina Press, 1965), 3–31, Drew Hyland, "Why Plato Wrote Dialogues," *Philosophy and Rhetoric* (1968), 38–50, Rudolph H. Weingartner, *The Unity of the Platonic Dialogue* (Indianapolis: Bobbs-Merrill, 1973), and Ronald Hathaway, "Explaining the Unity of the Platonic Dialogue," *Philosophy and Literature* 8 (1984), 195–208. I take it for granted, as virtually all of these people do, that the dialogues are characterized by a unity of form and content. For an opposing view, see Josiah B. Gould, "Klein on Ethological Mimes, for example, the *Meno*," *Journal of Philosophy* 66 (1969), 253–65. In regard to the *Meno*, the specifics of my disagreement with Klein and Gould will be spelled out in Chapter Seven below.

3. Vlastos, "The Paradox of Socrates," in Vlastos (ed.), *The Philosphy of Socrates* (Garden City, N.J.: Doubleday, 1971), 12.

4. Tarrant, *op. cit.*, 28.

5. R. Hackforth, *Plato's Phaedrus* (Cambridge: Cambridge University Press, 1952), 158.

6. Later, at 276b ff. Socrates suggests that writing is a frivolous activity comparable to the hasty planting of shrubs and repeats his basic criticism: that written words cannot defend themselves. Socrates' attack on the written word has led some scholars to conclude that Plato's real thought was transmitted orally so that rather than looking to the dialogues, we should try to construct it from other sources, in particular Aristotle. As far as I am concerned, this view was refuted once and for all by Harold Cherniss in *The Riddle of the Early Academy* (Berkeley and Los Angeles:

University of California Press, 1945). But it has resurfaced in the writings of K. Gaiser, *Platons Ungeschriebene Lehre* (Stuttgart: W. Kohlhammer, 1963) and H. J. Krämer, *Arte bei Platon und Aristoteles* (Heidelberg: Abhandlungen Heidelberger Akademie, 1959). For a review of Kramer, see Vlastos, "On Plato's Oral Doctrine," *Gnomon* 41 (1963), 641–55. The esoteric view is also defended by J. N. Findlay in Plato: *The Written and Unwritten Doctrines* (London: Routledge & Kegan Paul, 1974). See, in particular, 19–20, where Findlay claims that Plato's teaching ". . . cannot have been confined to a study of the Dialogues, on which in fact it seems that Plato commented little, though some like the *Phaedo*, and later the *Timaeus*, were closely studied. But the whole gist and thrust of Plato's main thinking is not to be found in the Dialogues taken alone, however much some have tried to find it there. The Dialogues themselves (for example *Phaedrus*, 275–6) proclaim the superiority of oral over written exposition, the latter consisting of words that resemble life-like paintings that maintain an august silence when interrogated, and are unable to defend themselves if attacked or abused, whereas the former create living 'writings' in the soul, that are able to speak for and defend themselves. And the Dialogues themselves constantly refer to a more thorough treatment that must occur 'elsewhere,' and would be hollow productions were these promises themselves hollow. Thus Socrates in the *Republic* says (506) that he must 'now leave the question as to what the Good Itself is, for it seems to be beyond my present powers to bring out what I have in mind on the present occasion,' or that, despite all effort, a great deal is being left out and must be left out in the development of the likeness of the Sun (509c). The whole account of the Good in the *Republic*, in fact, points to a missing elucidation, and is unintelligible without it, and so do such statements as that about the soul as being something whose uniformity or triformity can only be established by methods more accurate than those followed in the Dialogues (435d, 612a). The missing elucidation is, however, largely available, even if it itself demands further elucidation. . ." In contrast to Findlay, I do not see why Plato's words in the *Republic* or anywhere else are unintelligible without an esoteric doctrine which must be reconstructed from a variety of texts. To point out the limitations of the written word, to warn against passive acceptance of philosophic truths, is not necessarily to imply that one has a separate body of truth which is being withheld from the reader.

7. See *Gorgias* 447c, 449c, *Protagoras* 329a ff., *Euthydemus* 275a, *Hippias Major* 282b–c.

8. Friedländer, *Plato: An Introduction*, translated by H. Meyerhoff (New York, Bollingen, 1958), 166.

9. *Meno* 81d, 82a, 84d, 85d. Compare these references with Socrates' frequent skepticism about the teaching of virtue, e.g., *Apology* 20a–c, *Laches* 186a ff., and *Protagoras* 319a ff. By "teach" in these passages, Socrates

may have in mind the teaching methods of the sophists. That leaves open the question of whether teaching is possible in a different sense, i.e., elenctic teaching. This issue will be taken up in Chapters Six and Seven.

10. Klein, *op. cit.*, 7.

11. Klein, *op. cit.*, 20.

12. Randall, *Plato: Dramatist of the Life of Reason* (New York: Columbia University Press, 1977), 122. A less extreme version of this position can be found in Merlan, ibid. I agree with Merlan that "The form of Plato's writings attracts and repels at the same time," 429. I will develop this theme below. But I think Merlan goes too far when he says that Plato "never communicated what was essential to him." Surely the issues Socrates talks about were essential to Plato and the stands Socrates takes, ones which Plato sought to recommend. We can admit, with Merlan, that the dialogues leave us cross-examined rather than instructed without positing an absolute and ineffable truth which lies behind them. All we have to say is that the dialogue form allows for the possibility of genuine discovery on the part of the reader.

13. Rudolph Weingartner, *op. cit.*, 5.

14. Letters of John Keats, selected by F. Page (London: Oxford University Press, 1954), 53. Cited in Weingartner, *op. cit..*, 4.

15. Vlastos, *op. cit.*, 7. In view of *Apology* 29d–e, 30a, and 36c, it is hard for me to understand how anyone could have argued that the purpose of *elenchus* is merely to point out inconsistencies in others. And if that evidence is insufficient, the text of the *Crito*, where Socrates uses *elenchus* to argue that it is better for him to remain in prison, ought to be decisive. But this position was argued by Grote, *Plato and the Other Companions of Socrates* Vol. I (London: John Murray, 1875), 236–77, 281 ff. and Vlastos in his introduction to the *Protagoras* (Indianapolis: Bobbs-Merrill, 1956). It has since been rejected by Vlastos in "The Socratic Elenchus," in J. Annas (ed.), *Oxford Studies in Ancient Philosophy* (Oxford: Clarendon Press, 1983), 27–58. For further comment on Vlastos' paper, see Richard Kraut's paper in the same volume. I agree with Kraut that Vlastos puts entirely too much emphasis on *Gorgias* 479e, which is hardly the place where Socrates thinks he has a positive moral result. The price one pays for thinking that the purpose of *elenchus* is merely to expose inconsistency is that Socrates becomes something of a dogmatist. If, as the dialogues clearly show, he had deep moral convictions, and if *elenchus* could not be used to support them, on what basis did Socrates think they were true?

16. Burnyeat, "Virtues in Action," in Vlastos (ed.), *The Philosophy of Socrates, op. cit.*, 213.

17. Cf. Terence Irwin, *Plato's Moral Theory* (Oxford: Clarendon Press, 1977), 40: ". . . a disclaimer of knowledge does not require a disclaimer of all positive convictions." Failure to see this point destroys the uniqueness of Socrates' position. Anyone can disclaim knowledge if he has no real con-

victions about how to live a life. What makes Socrates' position so interesting is that he *had* such convictions and disclaimed knowledge anyway. At *Gorgias* 509a, he claims to have arguments of adamant and steel that his view of moral life is correct; but earlier, at 506a, he explicitly disclaimed knowledge (cf. *Republic* 354b). There is, however, one passage in the *Apology* which appears to contradict this. At 29b, Socrates says he *does* know that it is disgraceful to do wrong and disobey one's superior. Does this negate what he says in the rest of the *Apology*, the *Gorgias*, and elsewhere? I believe it does not. The use of *know* at *Apology* 29b is referring to the strength of Socrates' moral commitment. This does not mean, nor does Socrates ever say, that his belief follows from a completed moral theory or science. He is committed to it even though he cannot give a totally satisfactory justification for it. Such commitment would be objectionable only if it led Socrates to say either (1) that he refuses to subject it to further scrutiny, or (2) that others must accept it on his authority. But he never says either one. This is esentially the view taken by Vlastos in "The Paradox of Scorates," *op. cit.*, 10–2. A very different view is defended by Richard Kraut in *Socrates and the State* (Princeton: Princeton University Press, 1984), 274–9. According to Kraut, Socrates' position in the *Apology* is different from that found in later dialogues like the *Meno*. In the *Apology*, Socrates cannot define justice but thinks he knows something about it: that it is wrong to disobey a superior. In the *Meno* and elsewhere, he thinks that without a definition, such knowledge is impossible. Here we should note, as Kraut admits, that the evidence for putting the *Apology* among Plato's very early dialogues is inconclusive. Though it is often treated as an elementary text, it is a defense of Socrates' entire life and one of our best sources for understanding the elenctic process. In view of the fact that the *Apology* is a public oration, I see nothing untoward or insincere in Socrates' using *know* to mean "is strongly committed to" rather than "has the best possible grounds for asserting." True, this means Socrates is equivocating but (1) once understood, the equivocation is not harmful to his position, and (2) there is no reason to think that straight, univocal predication is always to be preferred. For these reasons, I side with Vlastos.

18. Grote, *op. cit.*, 291–2.
19. Grote, *op. cit.*, 291–2.
20. The tone of this passage stands in marked contrast to that of *Phaedo* 66b–67b. On the other hand, the *Meno* passage occurs in a conttext which assumes multiple incarnations so that the discovery of "all the rest" may require more than one lifetime. Cf. *Philebus* 24d.
20. Nietzsche, *The Birth of Tragedy*, translated by W. Kaufman (New York: Random House, 1976), 97.
21. I owe this insight to Robert Brumbaugh. For a similar analysis of the *Laches*, see Michael J. O'Brien, "The Unity of the *Laches*." in Anton and

Kustan (eds.), *Essays in Ancient Greek Philosophy* (Albany: SUNY Press, 1971), 303–315.

22. Kierkegaard, *Philosophical Fragments*, originally translated by D. F. Swenson, translation revised by H. W. Hong (Princeton: Princeton University Press, 1962), 75–6.

23. I agree with Irwin, against Dodds, that this passage still leaves open the possibility that Callicles, or someone like him, can be reached through rational argument: "If we thoroughly examine the same issues often and better, Callicles, you'll be persuaded." See Irwin, *Plato: Gorgias* (Oxford: Clarendon Press, 1979), 233. In fact, as Irwin points out, this passage calls to mind *Meno* 85c, where Socrates suggests the slave can obtain as good a knowledge of geometry as anyone else if questions are put to him over and over. But the fact that Callicles *could* be reached by rational argument only heightens the tragedy that, in fact, he will not be. In Chapter Seven, I will use a similar line of argument in regard to Meno: contrary to Klein, he is not depraved and could learn about virtue if he stayed in Athens and submitted to Socratic questioning. But the audience knows that none of this happened.

24 Knox, *Oedipus at Thebes* (New York: W. W. Norton, 1957), 51.

25. This theme, that Socrates is the loyal servant of Apollo is continued in the *Phaedo* 60d, 61b, 85b. It is the essence of Socrates' conception of himself as a religious hero and will be discussed in greater detail in Chapter Four.

26. Nietzsche, *op. cit.*, 89. Compare Xenophon's *Memorabilia* 4.3.2: " . . . no one in human memory ever bore death in a nobler way. He was forced to live for 30 days after he was sentenced . . . During that time, as every one of his associates could see, he lived as he had lived before."

27. Nietzsche, *op. cit.*, 91.

28. Friedländer, *op. cit.*, 158.

Chapter Two
Dialogue and the Search for Essence

I N THE PREVIOUS CHAPTER we saw that for Plato the dialogue form is uniquely suited to philosophical inquiry because it does not force the author to deliver a monologue. To this it might be added that human reflection is by nature a dialectical activity. As Richard Nettleship once claimed: "A process analogous to that of questioning others goes on in the mind of a single inquirer."[1] If Nettleship is right, we can understand why Plato frequently describes thinking as a dialogue the mind carries on with itself.[2] In this way, conversation becomes a paradigm. Even when one is engaged in silent reflection, the model Plato looks to is that in which two people secure agreement before moving ahead. It is unfortunate that in the subsequent history of philsophy, *dialectic* came to stand for a variety of thought patterns, many of which are really monologues. In a Platonic context, it is not enough to have a thesis, antithesis, and synthesis: there must be people willing to defend them.[3] In the *Gorgias* 447a) and *Protagoras* (328d), monologue or *epideiksis* is associated with sophistry.

1. THINKING AS A SOCIAL ACTIVITY

The above view of mental activity reinforces the notion that the subject of philosophic inquiry is a moral agent. Thought is a form of conversation, and conversation, as Richard Robinson pointed out, is a social activity.[4] To follow Robinson's point, thought is understood in terms of speech. But genuine speech requires more than linguistic competence. Arrogance, conceit, and hostility—all the vices which threaten social harmony also threaten conversation. To the degree that they threaten conversation, they hinder philosophical discovery. Thus Plato claims in the *Seventh Epistle* (344b) that it is only when people ask and answer questions in a spirit of benevolence and without

23

envy that philosophical discovery (*eklampsis*) can take place.[5] On the conversational model, then, thought always involves a moral component.

Such a view of philosophy is by no means universal. Aristotle argues in the *Sophistical Refutations* that we are more prone to fallacy and error when we use speech as the model for thought.[6] For Aristotle, dialectic is inferior to demonstration (*apodeiksis*). In demonstration, one begins with principles which are true and primary; that is, principles whose truth is known immediately and is not derived from other things (*Posterior Analytics* 71b20 ff.). It may be said, therefore, that Aristotle looked to mathematics for his model, not to Socratic conversations.[7] In a Socratic conversation, true and primary principles are the outcome of the intellectual process, never the starting point. Truth is something the participants in the discussion seek out. The starting point is the body of opinion the respondent brings to the discussion. But these opinions are not starting points in the sense that their truth is taken for granted; they are not premises. Rather, they are things to be examined and, if need be, overturned.[8]

The key point is that Socratic conversation forces one to deal with another person while demonstration does not. No matter how alien the other person's opinion may seem, or how certain one's own, a Socratic discussion cannot move forward until something has been accepted by both parties. As Socrates says to Crito in the midst of an urgent plea to escape from prison (49d–e):

> For I know that there are few people who do or ever will believe what I have said. Those who believe it and those who do not have no common ground on which to make a decision. Looking at each other's opinion, they are forced to regard the other person with contempt. So please consider very carefully whether you are with me and agree with me in this matter, so that we can take as a starting point the assumption that it is never right to do a wrong or to return one wrong for another or to prevent evil by doing it to someone else. Or do you disagree and not stand with me on this assumption? I have long believed it and do now, but if you have a different view, speak and explain it to me.

As we saw in the previous chapter, Socrates often refers to *elenchus* as a kind of persuasion.[9]

By *persuasion* is meant that the *elenchus* is not aimed at a general audience but at the individual respondent: its purpose is to get *him* to change his mind. As Robinson points out, the art of *elenchus* is to find premises which the respondent believes but which entail the abandonment of his original thesis.[10] That is why, according to Robinson, Polus has trouble conducting an elenctic examination of Socrates: he can identify premises which everyone else believes, but unless Socrates himself believes them, *Socrates* does not have to abandon anything he said. It follows that elenctic examination does not allow appeals to popular opinion or to outside authorities.[11] As Socrates tells Polus (*Gorgias* 472b–c): "If I do not produce in you yourself a single witness who agrees with what I say, in my view I have accomplished nothing of value in regard to whatever we might be discussing. Nor, in my view, have you accomplished anything of value if you do not produce me as your sole witness and forget all the others." Because the goal of *elenchus* is to persuade the individual respondent, all that matters is what the respondent is willing to accept.

But if this is so, *elenchus* is open to an objection. As Robinson put it: "The Socratic elenchus is a very personal affair, in spite of Socrates' ironical declarations that it is an impersonal search for truth."[12] This raises a serious question: How is the search for truth to proceed? Should one begin with a particular person and demand that she say what she really thinks or with principles designed to appeal to everyone? The danger of the first approach is what Robinson terms particularity and accidentalness. A questioner and respondent may agree to something without bothering to ask *why*. In this case, their agreement can harldly be said to constitute knowledge. To take the criticism one step further, the respondent is refuted when he agrees to something which contradicts his original thesis and comes to recognize the contradiction. The reader is an onlooker. Suppose, however, that the reader does not wish to accept what the respondent does. Or, suppose the reader thinks there is an obvious point the respondent has missed. Under these circumstances, the reader is likely to feel shortchanged. In a strict sense, all that happened is that a particular character in a dialogue failed the test of elenctic examination. The danger of the second approach is that the general reader is nothing but an abstraction which allows the author to put forward views in a dogmatic way. To his credit, Robinson does not hide his feelings and asserts that Socratic *elenchus* " . . . is inferior to the impersonal and universal and rational march of a science axiomatized according to Aristotle's prescription." The real question, then, is, as Robinson sees, why the Socratic method is needed for philosophical discovery.[13] Even if we grant that Socratic method is directed more to the discovery of truth than to its communication, we must ask why it is necessary for discovery. It is to this question that the present chapter is addressed.

2. SOCRATIC ESSENTIALISM

The first line of response to Robinson is to point out that the subject matter of Socratic philosophy does not lend itself to axiomatization. To put it bluntly, Socratic philosophy tries to reason *to* axioms rather than *from* them. The fundamental quest of Socratic philosophy is to answer the question "What is it?" This question is paramount in the *Euthyphro, Laches, Charmides, Lysis, Hippias Major, Meno,* and *Republic* I. But even in dialogues like the *Gorgias* and *Protagoras*, it is not far from view.[14] In the *Republic* (511, 533–4), Socrates argues that one of the things which distinguishes dialectic from the other sciences is that it alone tries to give an account of what each thing is.[15] If we were to compare a Socratic dialogue with an axiomatized science, we would find more than a difference in presentation. In Euclid, for example, the definitions are stated at the beginning. There is no mention of how they were derived or what, if anything, are the alternatives. Although we can imagine someone asking "What is a circle?" or "What is a square?" these questions would not arise in the normal course of geometric reasoning unless someone were learning it for the first time. If a mathematician were to ask these questions, we would probably conclude that something was wrong with Euclidean geometry so that serious revision was in order. This is exactly the point of Socrates asking his "What is it?" question in the way he does: to bring about serious revision.

Obviously such revision cannot be settled by demonstration. We would want to know what consequences to expect if we adopted a new definition of circle or square, but the search for a new definition, and the decision of whether to accept it, is not amenable to demonstrative solution. Demonstration takes us *from* first principles *to* specific conclusions; as long as the first principles are in doubt, it can show connections between propositions but cannot establish truth. Here Aristotle is in agreement: a demonstration cannot tell us what something is; it can only tell us what things are true of it.[16] Once the principles of geometry are accepted, we can demonstrate that a triangle must have interior angles equal to 180 degrees. But no demonstration can show how triangle must be defined.

If the answer is not found in demonstration, neither is it found in induction.[17] We normally think of induction as a process of moving from the specific to the general. Yet it is well known that Socrates does not allow his respondents to proceed in this way. When his respondents provide a list of examples or a description of highly specific criteria, he objects. The objection revolves around the fact that for Socrates, knowledge of a thing's essence is prior to any other knowledge about it, including the knowledge of what things exemplify it. In the *Euthyphro* (6e), Socrates wants to know what holiness is so that using it as a standard, he can decide what things are holy and what things are not.[18] The implication is that unless we can agree on such a standard, there would be no rational way of making this decision: if *X* is a disputed term, and you do not know what it is, you cannot know whether a specific description qualifies as *X* or not. Here we would do well to consider the context in which Socrates' question arises. It is not that left to their own devices, people can agree on what counts as an example of *X* but that when pressed to formulate a definition, they experience trouble. If that were the case, examination of individual cases or highly specific criteria might be a plausible way of answering Socrates' question.

The *Euthyphro* presupposes a situation in which the identification of individual cases is very much in dispute. Both Euthyphro and Socrates are involved in a court case involving piety: Euthyphro as prosecutor, Socrates as defendant. Both cases are controversial. A person who argued that we can formulate a definition of piety by looking at such cases would thus be guilty of begging the question. Suppose there is a dispute on whether prosecuting one's father for murder qualifies as a pious act. It will not do to derive a definition from this or related examples and reply that it does. As R. E. Allen put it: " . . . if your criterion rules out my example, I may reject my example, but I may equally reject your criterion—much will depend, no doubt, on whose ox is gored. If the only appeal in moral argument is to criteria of use extracted from examples, Euthyphro and his father are each in a logically impregnable position."[19]

It may be objected that one cannot derive a definition of a disputed term from an examination of individual cases if those cases are as controversial as Euthyphro's prosecution of his father. But what about cases which do not normally arouse such controversy? Could we not agree, for example, that Achilles or the Athenian soldiers at Marathon were courageous and use them as paradigms? The problem with this suggestion is its appeal to popular opinion. When Laches objects that Nicias's definition of courage excludes wild animals and other commonly recognized examples, Nicias replies, apparently with Socrates' approval, that popular opinion is based on a false understanding because it does not distinguish courage, which is a moral quality, from rashness, which is not (196e–197c).[20] That is, Nicias refuses to accept examples which most people would regard as clear-cut. The rules of *elenchus* permit him to do this as long as the examples he does accept are consistent with the definition he has proposed.

Or, to take another passage, consider Meno's first definition of virtue:

> First of all, if you want to know about the virtue of a man, that's easy: the virtue of a man consists in competent management of the affairs of the city, helping one's friends, harming his enemies, and seeing to it that he comes to no harm himself. Or, if you want to know about the virtue of a women, that, too, is easy to say: she must manage her house well, taking care of her possessions, and being obedient to her husband. There's a different virtue for children, whether male or female, and for the aged, free or slave, as you like.

From the standpoint of conventional morality, Meno is not saying anything controversial. He is not prosecuting anyone, and at this stage in his life, has no one prosecuting him. Yet as any reader of the dialogue soon learns, the categories Meno regards as important, chiefly race, sex, and social class, having nothing to do with virtue. Meno's problem is not a failure to deal with controversial cases, but something more radical: a failure to recognize the true standards for assessing a person's life.

It happens that Meno does not cite specific examples of virtue in the opening pages of the dialogue, but if he had, they would have been men who secured political power and used it to their own advantage. Sooner or later these examples would have been rejected because they reflect the materialistic values Socrates wanted people to give up.[21] Socrates' quest for definitions is not motivated by a simple concern for cleaning up language or clarifying terms. The picture which emerges from the dialogues is one in which society's values seem to be falling apart. In the *Euthyphro* (7c ff.), we are told that there is no end of debate on moral questions and that even the gods have trouble agreeing with one another. In the *Gorgias* we see an articulate and well educated Athenian maintain that the morality of the day is false and hypocritical and that nature herself ordains that only the powerful should rule. A similar view is advanced by a well known sophist in *Republic* I. Add to this the failure of the Athenian statesmen to look after the education of their sons, Polus' admiration for the archcriminal Archelaus, the pervasive hypocrisy discussed by Glaucon and Adeimantus in *Republic* II, and we can begin to understand why Socrates is reluctant to take popular opinion for granted. Again, serious revision is in order.

More important, we must keep in mind the tragic dimension of Socratic philosophy discussed in the first chapter. Many of the characters we see eventually meet with disaster. If we take Thucydides seriously, there is a sense in which all of fifth century Greece met with disaster because it plunged itself into a long and bitter conflict. The deterioration of moral standards, in particular the ability to understand the basic terms of moral discourse, is described by Thucydides in a passage dealing with civil strife in Corcyra.[22]

> To fit in with the change of events, words, too, had to change their usual meanings. What used to be described as a thoughtless act of agression was now regarded as the courage one would expect to find in a party member; to think of the future and wait was merely another way of saying one was a coward; any idea of moderation was just an attempt to disguise one's unmanly character; ability to understand a question from all sides meant one was totally unfitted for action. Fanatical enthusiasm was the mark of a real man, and to plot against an enemy behind his back was perfectly legitimate self-defense.

In such an environment, even the judgment that Achilles is courageous would be subject to examination. Was this an isolated occurrence? The plague at Athens, the reign of Cleon, the massacres at Melos and Mycalessus, the treatment of the Athenian prisoners at Syracuse, and the rule of the Thirty Tyrants suggest it was not. All of these events took place during Socrates' adult life.

What does this have to do with the search for essence? The answer is that if something at the heart of Athenian society has gone wrong so that commonly accepted judgments cannot be trusted, simple induction is insufficient to answer the question Socrates is asking. Since the purpose of seeking a definition is to *resolve* conflicts which have arisen in the classification of individual cases, generalizing from such cases accomplishes nothing.

But if induction will not work because it begs the question, and demonstration will not work because we have not yet identified the principles from which to derive consequences, what will? To put this a different way, since induction presupposes agreement on individual cases, and demonstration presupposes agreement on first principles, neither is flexible enought to allow the revision Socrates seems to want.[23] Such freedom is a crucial part of elenctic examination: the respondent must always be permitted to strike out in a radically new direction. Hence the constant refrain: Do not worry about what other people believe, say what *you* think. The question is how Socrates can preserve such freedom and still search for definitions in a systematic way. Before tackling this quesiton, however, it is necessary to clear-up some possible misunderstandings.

3. TWO QUALIFICATIONS

In assessing the character of Socrates' position, we must keep in mind that there are two things he is *not* committed to. To claim that we cannot *derive* a definition from a set of examples is not to claim that we cannot use examples to persuade the respondent to change his mind.[24] When Laches defines courage as staying at one's post (190e), Socrates objects that the Scythians are deemed courageous even though they fight in retreat. Laches accepts this example and is forced to modify his definition. Although Laches cannot *know* that Scythians are courageous until he has defined courage, his belief that they are forces him to change his position. The questioner can appeal to such beliefs in an attempt to get the respondent to achieve consistency. The point is that until the respondent has arrived at an acceptable definition, they are *only* beliefs. Another way to put this is that the acceptance of examples is provisional until the respondent has discovered a theory for dealing with them. Laches accepts the Scythian fighters as a legitimate example of courage and modifies his position accordingly. But there is nothing to prevent him from abandoning this example at a later stage if he becomes committed to a definition which excludes it.

Peter Geach has objected that one can look for a definition if there is agreement on examples, or can look for examples if there is agreement on a defintion, but that one cannot proceed if there is agreement on neither one.[25] But surely Geach has imposed an unduly severe requirement on moral thinking. There is no reason why we cannot leave both questions open and try to achieve coherence by bringing each into harmony with the other. And even if such harmony is achieved, we may still want to insist on the freedom to make revisions. As John Rawls put it:[26]

> Moral philosophy is Socratic: we may want to change our
> present considered judgments once their regulative principles
> are brought to light. And we may want to do this even
> though these principles are a perfect fit. A knowledge of these
> principles may suggest further reflections that lead us to
> revive our judgments. This feature is not peculiar though to
> moral philosophy, or to the study of other philosophical prin-
> ciples such as those of induction and scientific method.

So there is nothing wrong with provisionality in either direction.

The Socratic insistence on the priority of definition is not intended to exclude any mention of examples but to prevent the sort of position adopted by Justice Stewart when he made his famous remark about pornography: I can't define it, but I know it when I see it. Without a principle to justify the claim that something is pornographic, Stewart could not establish a set of reasonable guidelines. In the absence of a general criterion, the Court let local communities make their own judgments.

The second thing Socrates is not committed to is the claim that a definition can settle moral disputes all by itself. There is a tendency to think of definitions along the line of the entries found in a dictionary, i.e., as isolated statements offering verbal equivalences. It is fantastic to suppose that such equivalences could resolve the deep-seated moral disputes Socrates is talking about. We can, therefore, agree with Richard Kraut when he says:[27]

> [Socrates] can hardly be criticized for thinking that all he
> needs is one magical sentence about the virtues (or perhaps a
> separate one for each), and suddenly perfection will be
> achieved. Rather, he must believe that the search for a proper
> account of the virtues will require the discovery of a large
> number of moral truths, and that after we systematically ex-
> plore these truths, we will be able to single out one statement
> about virtue (or perhaps one corresponding to each virtue)
> that will serve as our definition. That definition will form the
> most important part of our new theory, but it need not be
> understandabale apart from its relation to all the rest.

To return to Stewart, a definition of pornography will be acceptable only if it is accompanied by a series of moral and aesthetic claims, not to mention a body of legal rules and practises. That is why it makes little sense to refer to such definitions as analytic. If the discovery of a correct account of pornography, or virtue, raises a host of collateral issues which take us well into areas like moral psychology or public policy, it is fruitless to insist that the resulting definition is true by virtue of the meaning of its terms.[28]

In the *Meno*, the question "What is virtue?" takes the participants into such diverse areas as logic (73e–75a), moral psychology (77b–78b), epistemology (80d ff.), and ordinary value judgments (73a–c). So the correct definition would be the foundation for a wide range of judgments and conclusions—to paraphrase Nicias, of an entire outlook on life. To treat the definition in isolation from these judgments and conclusions and suppose that all Socrates wants is a sentence or two is to trivialize his motivation for demanding a definition in the first place.

4. DEFINITION AND REFUTATION

With these qualifications in mind, we may return to the central question: How is the search for definitions to proceed and why is the method of question and answer necessary? Note that the search we are talking about is not the sort involved in finding a cure for cancer. In asking "What is courage?" or "What is piety?" Socrates is not inquiring about an esoteric subject. Courage and piety are concepts presupposed by ordinary moral judgments. As such, they are concepts about which Socrates' respondents already have an opinion.[29] We have seen that there is no single inference to take one to the knowledge Socrates is after. In this respect, he is asking for a genuine discovery.

I submit that if there is no direct way of reasoning to a definition of moral quality, Socrates had no choice but to proceed *in*directly, by way of refutation.[30] If there is no inference guaranteed to lead us to the true definition, there is at least a way of knowing when we have a false one: a definition is false when it contradicts something else the respondent believes and, faced with the inconsistency, the respondent voluntarily gives it up. On this view, discovery is understood negatively: it is more a matter of discarding false ideas than of finding an unbroken path to the true one. A case in point is Socrates' examination of Meno's slave. Although the mathematical truth Socrates wants the boy to discover could be presented as a conclusion from premises, that is not how Socrates chooses to present it. The boy is presented with a puzzle: how to double the area of a square. From the information he is given, there is no inference which will take him to the right answer. Instead of moving from premises to conclusions, the boy is asked to put forward tentative proposals and subject them to criticism. He responds with an initial impression, and Socrates shows him it will not work. He tries another, and Socrates shows him it will not work either. When the boy runs out of ideas, Socrates offers a hint, but not until the boy has voluntarily given up a number of tempting suggestions and is ready to look for something else. This passage will be discussed in greater detail in a later chapter; for the present, note its underlying theme: knowledge advances when intellectual options are closed off.

The issue, then, is not whether the respondent can *derive* a correct definition from an existing set of beliefs—that is impossible—but whether he can articulate a definition *compatible* with those beliefs and accept the consequences to which it commits him. Put otherwise, discovery is furthered by helping the respondent to see what his own admissions prevent him from saying. That is why it is important that, like Meno's slave, the respondent has an opinion on the matter right from the start. The purpose of the examination is to help him remove the obstacles which prevent him from being perfectly satisfied with his own responses. Unless these responses are subjected to criticism, he will never know whether they express his real convictions. It may be said therefore that the more contradictions the questioner can expose, the faster the respondent will be able to learn what he himself wants to say. Thus Socrates tells Gorgias (458a) that it is better to *be* refuted than to refute someone else.

If it is asked how one will recognize when a true definition has been secured, the only answer is to carry elenctic examination to the point where criticism no longer requires the respondent to take anything back. In this connection, Socrates tells Callicles (*Gorgias* 487e) that any agreement between them would certainly constitute truth. This may seem odd since Socrates' remark occurs just after Callicles' brutal assault on the philosophic way of life. Socrates contends, however, that Callicles is the perfect respondent because he possesses all the necessary characteristics: intelligence, good will, and candor. The latter is the most important. Callicles is willing to say what he thinks even if it proves insulting. Socrates' reaction is not to take offense but to recognize that only with a person like Callicles can his beliefs really be put to the test (486d–e). Behind Socrates' attitude is an assumption according to which refutation must be as vigorous as possible if the search for truth is to have any hope of success. That is why the respondent cannot put forth hypotehticals or quote outside authorities. He himself must be completely committed to what he is saying. In the *Gorgias*, only Callicles fits this description (487b).

All of this is a way of saying that *elenchus* is a dramatic endeavor. In the *Republic* (534c), Socrates picks up on this point by claiming that the dialectician, whose job it is to uncover the essence of things, must be able to fight through all of the objections put to him and, as in battle, make his way without stumbling. Such a process can go on in the mind of a single person, but if discovery is facilitated by criticism, this situation is clearly derivative. Responding to one's own objections, or to those of a disciple, or even to those of "the general reader" do not count as putting one's beliefs to the test.

It is true, therefore, that *elenchus* is a personal affair. It is no better than the participants' willingness to speak frankly in criticizing other people's positions and respond graciously when their own positions are under attack. It is also true that the criticisms Socrates makes are often *ad hominem* in the sense that the respondents' answers must be consistent with their behavior. Gorgias and Protagoras are asked to defend the legitimacy of their life's work. In defense of Socrates, we may ask whether discovery can be anything *but* personal, particularly when moral issues are at stake.[31] The definition of a moral term like courage or justice is more than a statement of fact; it is also a recommendation for how to live. We cannot subject such recommendations to criticism without raising issues of personal integrity. Even in the sciences, we may question whether the growth of knowledge is totally impersonal or whether integrity and self interest also play a part. However impersonal the results of a science may seem once the initial ground has been broken, we have no right to assume that the defeat of old theories or the establishment of new ones do not present tests as difficult as those presented by Socrates.

In any case, refutation is not something Socrates picked up by accident. Since the "What is it?" question could not be answered by demonstration from premises or induction from particulars, there was no alternative but to criticize answers to which people were already committed in the hope that eventually a stable answer would emerge. Popper saw in Socrates the ideal of a person committed to critical discussion as a way of obtaining truth.[32] We must keep in mind, however, that Socrates was not doing cosmology; the Socratic commitment to criticism is a function of the Socratic search for essence. How Socrates would have proceeded in the realm of empirical science is anyone's guess.

5. REFUTATION AND RECOLLECTION

To the degree that refutation is its paradigm, Socratic method may be characterized as a struggle for consistency. The respondent can reject a definition that is incompatible with another belief or reject a belief that is incompatible with his definition. He has the freedom to revise or reject anything he wants provided he remains consistent with himself. As long as consistency is not achieved, revision must go on. But once it is, and further questioning cannot upset it, the examination is over. There is, however, an obvious objection to making consistency the criterion of truth. Could a person not be consistently wrong? Since the respondent takes responsibility for the discussion in the sense that he decides how to modify his position, Socratic *elenchus* is no better than the respondent's ability to discriminate right from wrong. How do we know that faced with a decision to abandon a definition or other belief, the respondent will make the right choice? Could he not abandon a true definition just as easily as a false one? And if he did, would he not be like Popper's mountain climber who reaches the summit in a dense fog and continues to move forward? If the respondent is just as likely to abandon the true definition as a false one, Socratic *elenchus* is a hit or miss affair, and once again, the charge of particularity and accidentalness will make itself felt.

The only way to answer this criticism is to assume that the respondent has enough understanding of virtue to be able to make reasonable discriminations if the right questions are put to him and he is relieved of the burden of having to satisfy popular opinion. In other words, it is to assume that a false answer to the "What is it?" question ultimately will conflict with an intuition the questioner can arouse. Irwin is right to point out that the guiding principles of elenctic examination are not purely formal.[33] It is not merely that the respondent has the ability to see that if P implies Q, and Q implies not-R, that P and R are incompatible. He must have some understanding of the *content* of virtue, otherwise there is no reason to think that by answering questions about it, he will be led closer to the truth.

We can see this in a variety of ways. Depsite Meno's admiration for gold, silver, and high office, he cannot get himself to admit that a person can be virtuous no matter how he aquires them—even though he has to abandon two definitions as aresult (73d, 78d–e). And despite Callicles' contention that the attainment of pleasure is all that matters in a life, even *he* cannot accept everything it requires (*Gorgias* 494e ff. & 497e ff.). In short, Socratic philosophy cannot work unless it is impossible for someone to hold a consistent immoralism. That is why Socrates can say that as long as Callicles prefers doing injustice to suffering it, he will tie himself in knots.[34] If this were not true, if Callicles could revise his beliefs so that doing injustice were preferable to suffering it, *and if he could honestly accept the principles which justify such a view*, Socratic *elenchus* would be powerless against him. It follows that if *elenchus* is to be effective, the respondent must come to the discussion with intutitions a complete immoralist would have to reject. And this, in turn, is possible only if the respondent already has some idea of what virtue is.

If one were to push the criticism further and ask how it is possible for the respondent to have enough grasp of virtue to make inquiry worthwhile, he would bring us to the doorstep of the theory of recollection. All of this is possible because no matter how confused he may get, the respondent is never completely ignorant of what he is seeking. That is, no one is totally lacking in the moral intuitions needed to answer Socrates' questions.

Now the theory of recollection does not find its way into the dialogues until the *Meno*, and from a textual standpoint, there are no anticipations. We can speculate on whether the historical Socrates was aware of it or whether the credit should go to Plato. In either case, the important point is that the theory is needed if Socratic method is to have any hope of success. If the respondent were truly ignorant of virtue so that the questioner could not find any point of agreement, *elenchus* would never get started. I suggest, therefore, that by the time of the *Meno*, Plato came to realize what the conversational method was based on: principles which every rational person will agree to if given the opportunity to examine them. Once again, this makes *elenchus* a personal affair, but each person carries with her enough understanding of virtue to enable the inquiry to reach a positive result.

It follows that the inquiry is not just an on-going critique of current values. Socrates, the archetypical moralist, undertook it believing that there is a correct and incorrect way of defining virtue. The correct way is simply the one which allows the respondent to agree with himself, not only with the opinions he has expressed but with those he *would* express if he considered the matter thoroughly. Socrates does not explain this by appealing to conscience or shared moral experience. Since the foundation of a moral judgment is the definition of the moral quality in question, he explains it by claiming that knowledge of the definition must already be known to us in some way. If it were not, Socrates' confidence in the powers of *elenchus* would be completely misplaced.

6. METHOD AND MORALS

Elenchus is often called a *method* by Platonic scholars, and in one respect, it is. We have seen that there are rules dictating what the participants in the inquiry can and cannot do: (1) the respondent cannot hide behind hypotheticals, (2) the questioner cannot force the respondent to accept something he does not really believe, (3) the respondent has the freedom to make whatever modifications he wishes provided that he remains consistent with himself. But these rules do not constitute a *method* as that term is used by subsequent philosophers. There is nothing in the early dialogues corresponding to Aristotle's *Organon*, Descartes' *Rules for the Direction of the Mind*, or Husserl's phenomenological reduction. Our knowledge of *elenchus* is derived by watching Socrates in action. Vlastos is therefore correct in saying that Socrates never discusses the elenctic method *per se*.[35] He is interested in it only to the degree that clarifying this or that point allows him to continue talking about virtue. In this sense, there is a practical twist to everything Socrates says. When it comes to the all-important question of truth, there is little to say except: carry the method as far as it will go. The problem is that in the early dialogues, the method is never carried this far so that questions still remain.

The earliest passage which we could characterize as a self-conscious attempt to clarify method is *Meno* 86c–87c. The context is this. After failing to offer a satisfactory definition of virtue, Meno insists that they put off the question of what virtue is and return to the question of how it is acquired. The fact that Socrates had earlier warned against such a procedure (70b) does not phase Meno: he insists on doing things his way. Socrates agrees to go along but expresses strong reservations: "If I governed you, Meno, and not only myself, we would not consider whether or not virtue can be taught before first inquiring into what it is." The method for deciding whether virtue can be taught is borrowed from the geometers and consists of answering one question by reducing it to another. We may not know whether *P* is true. But if *Q* is a necessary and sufficient condition for *P*, we can decide the latter by answering the former. If *Q* is true, *P* is true; if not, then not.

In this way, the proposition "Virtue can be taught" is reduced to the proposition "Virtue is a kind of knowledge." If the latter is true, the former must be true as well. It happens that "Virtue is a kind of knowledge" is handled in a similar, though not quite identical, fashion.[36] It is said to follow from the proposition "Virtue is good" together with an argument to the effect that nothing is good unless it involves or is accompanied by knowledge. The overall conclusion is that virtue can be taught.

Although some scholars have seen in this passage an anticipation of dialectic, it is clear that Socrates adopts the method *reluctantly*.[37] This would be odd if it were something he was trying to recommend. Note, for example, that the method attempts to do what Socrates had earlier said cannot be done: it undertakes to tell us if virtue can be taught without first deciding what virtue is.[38] It is also worth noting that the conclusion it sanctions "Virtue can be taught" is soon over-turned on the grounds that it contradicts experience: despite repeated efforts to find someone who can teach virtue, Socrates has failed. Although the reason for overturning this conclusion is controversial, and will be discussed in a later chapter, as far as the *Meno* is concerned, the method borrowed from the geometers does not produce a stable result. This should hardly surprise us since geometry comes in for strong criticism in the *Republic* on just the grounds we would expect: like Meno, it attempts to avoid the "What is it?" question by putting derivative questions first.[39]

The first discussion of a method which could be described as Socrates' own does not come until *Phaedo* 99d–101e. There Socrates claims that his procedure consists in putting down the hypothesis he considers to be the strongest and determining what is and is not in accord with it. What is in accord he regards as true, and what is not he regards as false. If an hypothesis does not have any absurd or undesirable consequences, he looks for a more ultime hypothesis and repeats the procedure until he reaches something satisfactory. Unfortunately, Socrates' account of this procedure is exceedingly brief and has given rise to a number of technical problems.[40] But even if we could construct a clear idea of what he had in mind, we would face the problem that the method outlined in this passage takes us from one hypothesis to a higher one but never tells us how we eventually make the leap to an unhypothetical starting point, i.e., how we go from a tentative account of a moral term to the certainty that we have discovered its essential nature.

The same criticism could be made in regard to *Meno* 86c–87c. Both "Virtue can be taught" and "Virtue is a kind of knowledge" are supposed to follow from the hypothesis "Virtue is good."[41] But this most fundamental hypothesis is never subjected to examination. By what procedure could we go beyond it or any other hypothesis to the unhypothetical knowledge of what virtue is? The dialogue does not say.

Our expectations are heightened in the middle books of the *Republic* when Socrates is talking about dialectic. Although the context contains metaphysical assumptions which go beyond anything correctly described as Socratic, the search for essence is still of primary importance. Dialectic is the only science which gives an account of the essential nature of things and therefore the only science worthy of the name knowledge (533b–d). On the question of hypothesis, it is distinguished from geometry on the ground that it alone tries to go beyond hypotheses to something known with certainty (511a):

> It does not treat its hypotheses as first principles, but as hypotheses in the true sense of the word, namely as stepping stones and starting points in order to reach that which is beyond hypothesis, the first principle of everything that is.

Geometry, on the other hand, takes its hypotheses as starting points and never tries to justify them (510c). The result is that no matter how flawness the connection between these hypotheses and the theorems derived from them, geometry always retains the character of an if/then proposition.[42]

Yet even in the discussion of dialectic, what we get is not quite what we want. After being told that dialectic is a systematic way of discerning the essence of things, Glaucon asks for a fuller description of its nature, forms, and method (*Republic* 532d–e). But Socrates refuses, claiming that Glaucon would not be able to understand such a description for it would no longer be an image of what they are talking about but the reality. It is not clear what to make of this remark. Would an account of the nature, forms, and method of dialectic take him too far from the subject under discussion: the ideal state? Would

Glaucon be unable to understand it because he has not gone through the rigorous training required of the guardians? Is it impossible to give an account of dialectic without also giving an account of the things whose essence it apprehends? Or, is Plato once again calling attention to the limitations of the written word? We are not told.

From the admittedly incomplete account which follows, we can say this much. Dialectic constitutes an "upward path" in the sense that it does not ask what the hypotheses of the other sciences imply but seeks to determine what *would* imply them. That is, it moves from a given hypothesis to higher and higher hypotheses in an attempt to find something which is no longer an hypothesis at all but known to be true. Each time a new hypothesis is identified, consequences will have to be examined to insure that consistence has been maintained. This calls to mind the method outlined in the *Phaedo*. After examining the consequences of a tentative definition, the dialectician will modify her account of justice, piety, or courage and start over again. The process will continue until the element of tentativeness is lost. We can imagine that the dialectician will spend years criticizing and modifying her definition until the essence she is seeking has been identified. Cornford is right in saying that the entire description of dialectic in the *Republic* is phrased in the language of Socratic conversation.[43] As we saw before, the dialectician is an elenctic soldier who can fight off the objections put to her and remain on her feet. But this description is also short on details. Precisely how is certainty achieved? What must the dialectician do to make sure she has it? Can she train others to achieve the same thing? Again, we are not told.

The obvious conclusion is that even in the *Republic*, we do not get what contemporary philosophers would consider an adequate account of method. According to Robinson, Plato does not have in the *Republic* any more method at his disposal than he had in the *Phaedo*:[44]

> He merely claims that the man who competently and conscientiously practises this hypothetical and elenctic procedure will, or may, one day find himself in the possession of an unhypothetical certainty. He conceives that the dialectician takes an hypothesis and deduces its consequences, trying his hardest to discover some contradiction in those consequences. If he does discover one, the hypothesis is thereby refuted. He than takes another hypothesis, usually a modification of the first one designed to avoid the contradiction which refuted that. He then deduces the consequences of this second

hypothesis, again trying his hardest to make it a lead to a contradiction. He continues this process for a long time, making a
great effort to be patient and thorough. Some day, after
months or years of labour, he reflects that he has now been
attempting to refute the same hypothesis for many weeks,
and that this last hypothesis has endured every test and stood
consistent in all its consequences, which he has deduced on
every side as far as it seems possible to go. With this reflection (if he ever gets so far) it dawns on him that this
hypothesis is certainly true, that it is no longer an hypothesis
but an anhypotheton.

But this is tantamount to saying that certainty is achieved when *elenchus* is carried as far as it will go. As Robinson continues, we have
been given no reason to suppose that dialectic will achieve a non-
arbitrary certainty greater than that achieved by the other sciencs, in
particular mathematics. So we are back to Aristotle's criticism: the
conversational model is inferior to the deductive model of Euclid.

The answer to this criticism is that Socrates did not conceive of method
as a contemporary philosopher would. If an account of method is
supposed to be a series of procedures which can be taken up by any
reasonably intelligent person and followed to a successful conclusion,
then, I submit Socrates was opposed to method.[45] There are, of course,
long methodological passages in late dialogues like the *Sophist*,
Statesman, and *Philebus*. But despite vigorous scholarly debate on what
such methods involve, there is no reason to think these passages are accounts of what Socrates was doing all along. So even if it is true that
dialectic came to be identified with collection and division, we must keep
in mind that there is no hint of this method in a dialogue like the *Meno*.
Even in the *Republic*, the account of method is still too abbreviated for our
taste. Where we want greater detail on the specific steps the dialectician will take in isolating the essence of a moral quality, he provides
greater detail on the sort of *person* the dialectician will have to be. This
approach follows the lead of *Meno* 81c, where Socrates claims that recollection will work *if* we have the courage to pursue the investigatin. In the
passage from the *Seventh Epistle* referred to above, Plato denies that
quickness in learning or remembering are sufficient for philosophical
discovery.[46] There must be a kinship between the knower and the object she is trying to apprehend. Thus: "Knowledge never takes root
in an alien nature." A person not disposed to virtuous behavior will
never apprehend the essence of virtue, no matter how quick witted
she is.

Although the authenticity of the *Seventh Epistle* has been questioned, the idea that knowledge cannot take root in an alien nature is
a familiar one in the Platonic corpus.[47] That is why Socrates goes to such
great lengths to describe the training and education of the guardians,
warning on two occasions that dialectic may lead to harmful consequences if a person is introduced to it too early in life (498a, 537d ff.). So
whatever confidence he had in dialectic as a means of facilitating
discovery, he somehow thinks that the real question is the *people* who
can use it profitably. Perhaps that is the reason Socrates refuses to give
Glaucon, or the reader, a complete description: the method is of no
use to someone who is not ready to apprehend the things dialectic investigates. This sounds funny to us because we are not used to thinking of method from the standpoint of the person applying it. To take
an obvious example, if deduction is subject-neutral, it is also agent-
neutral. It requires technical facility but no particular moral exertion.
Not so with dialectic, which means that it is not a method in the usual
sense of the term.

We are back to the connection between morality and epistemology,
in particular the admission that due to the special nature of the search
on which Socrates was embarked, the "method" for obtaining truth
is no better than the agents' integrity in using it. That is why the
lengthy descriptions of musical and gymnastic training, military service, and social administration are not irrelevant. Virtue is not only the
object of the search but a determining factor in its success. If it takes
perseverance to learn about courage, fairness to learn about justice
etc., then the dialectician must exhibit the quality she is trying to
discover. Put otherwise, the discovery, like the process which
precedes it, is always in some measure *ad hominem*. A person lacking
in virtue will also lack the wherewithall needed to arrive at a proper
understanding of it. That brings us to the issue of certainty.

Robinson is right to the degree that the *Republic* does not have a
satisfactory account of method as *we* understand it. In the last
analysis, the upward path of dialectic culminates in a kind of intuition; as Robinson expresses it, it does not demonstrate the existence
of anything except in the sense in which raising the curtain
demonstrates the existence of the stage.[48] So the purpose of dialectic
is not to demonstrate the existence of things as much as it is to put us
in a position where we can command a clear perspective on them. It is
therefore a pathway (*hodos*) to a philosophical stance rather than a

way of certifying the truth of various propositions. Such a view of philosophical discovery will always be open to the charge of arbitrariness: How can we be sure that anyone who submits to the training Socrates describes and participates in the process of question and answer will one day see the same stage?

We cannot because the description of philosophical discovery, and the resulting kinship between knower and object known, are tied up with assumptions subsequent thinkers do not necessarily share: Socrates' distrust of teaching, Plato's distrust of the written word, the priority of essence, and the theory of recollection. Take away any of these assumptions and the conversational model will not stand up to Robinson's objections. Again, we can question whether the march of science is as impersonal as he suggests, whether actual progress is more a matter of looking for mistakes and responding to criticism than of moving from premises to conclusions, but no matter: Socrates neither was nor claimed to be a scientist. His overriding concern was practical. The search for essence is a way of getting people to examine their lives, which, in turn, is a way of getting them to live better ones. We can therefore imagine Socrates objecting to any method which does not take moral improvement seriously. He would no doubt object that if our conception of philosophical inquiry has become so depersonalized that it ignores the moral standing of the people engaged in it, then we have lost sight of what philosophy is supposed to be. In this respect, Socrates has more in common with the radio dial preacher than he does with the modern professor of philosophy.

To return to the *Republic*, certainty, if it comes at all, will come to very few people, and then only at an advanced age. It will be objected that stressing the difficulty of acquiring certainty does not answer the fundamental question of *how* it is acquired. True enough, but Socrates would reply that there is no philosophical formula or method which can describe the path to certainty in a way which abstracts from the subject matter. If a description were available, then, to paraphrase *Republic* 532d, we would no longer be describing the path but taking it. If this opens him to the charge of arbitrariness, he would only reply that it is a charge with which he is prepared to live as long as people recognize that the certainty he is talking about is not that which attaches to isolated propositions, sense impressions, or the inner workings of one's mind. Like all thought, dialectic is a social activity: it cannot advance until both the questioner and the respondent have given consent.

7. A SISYPHEAN DILEMMA

This chapter has investigated the conversational model of philosophy which underlies the Socratic dialogues and shapes Plato's understanding of dialectic. This conversational model is connected with two features of Socratic philosophy, one having to do with its subject matter, the other with its goal or purpose. The subject matter is Socrates' quest for definitions of moral terms; the goal or purpose, his conviction that philosophical inquiry is a way of helping people to improve the quality of their lives. To the degree that subsequent thinkers do not share these views, the conversational model will seem less than compelling. Along these lines, both features of Socratic philosophy are open to question.

Simply stated, the search for essence is a search for a rational way of resolving moral disputes. It assumes that problems which arise in everyday situations, e.g., Euthyphro's prosecution of his father, reflect deeper level problems about the qualities described by moral terms. The question of whether there are any essences in Socrates' sense is the question of whether an account of piety, courage, or justice can provide the foundation for a theory strong enough to answer philosophical questions and detailed enough to provide practical assistance. If the early dialogues prove anything, it is not just that the average Athenian did not go around with such a theory in his pocket. That no one would have disputed. It is that the job of providing one is much more difficult than it first appears.

The problem is not just that a definition must be sufficiently general to cover all legitimate examples—although that problem proves difficult enough for most of Socrates' respondents. Even if we have a formula of sufficient generality, (1) it must have explanatory power: thus "what all the gods love" cannot be the definition of piety because it does not tell us *why* they love it, (2) it must be clear why the quality so identified is good for us: Socrates typically assumes that the virtues are noble things,[49] (3) it must be clear how the virtue under discussion is related to other virtues and to the whole of virtue: Socrates rejects Nicias's definition of courage on the ground that it confuses part with whole, (4) the definition must be specific enough to help us in resolving everyday disputes otherwise there would be no point in seeking a definition in the first place.

It may be said, therefore, that Socrates raised forever the standards of what a rational solution to a moral dispute would have to be. As a general rule, his respondents do not come close to providing the information he needs. As Kraut has shown, even the claim "Virtue is knowledge" is a long way from satisfying these demands.[50] Knowledge is itself a disputed term and one whose definition is likely to raise many of the questions raised by virtue. Moreover there is no obvious way in which the equation of virtue with knowledge would assist a statesman, judge, or general in making elementary decisions. It follows that we should not be misled by the brevity of the "What is it?" question or the abruptness with which it is posed. Nor should we be misled into thinking that Socrates has the necessary information but has decided to keep it to himself. The Socratic dialogues are spurs to inquiry in the sense that they engage the reader and encourage her to think for herself.[51] But they are not like mystery novels where the author leaves a trail of clues pointing to a single conclusion. "What is justice?" cannot be answered in the way we answer "Who killed the butler?" We have the entire text of the *Republic* as proof.[52] So there is nothing insincere in Socrates' professing ignorance even though he has spent a lifetime examining the relation between virtue and knowledge. To complete his search, he would need logical, psychological, and metaphysical insights unavilable to any person in the fifth century.

But if this is so, Socratic essentialism is difficult to assess. If he had accounts of the virtues with which he was satisfied, we could attack or defend them as we see fit. But Socrates is the first to admit he does not have them, and at *Apology* 23a–b, he doubts whether any living person ever will. Although *he* does not make this point, we might support his assessment of human capabilities by saying that with new insights come new questions. If knowledge requires certainty in the sense that *elenchus* no longer exposes the need for revision, it may be that knowledge is all but inaccessible. In any case, Socratic philosophy does not offer us a body of results in the way that history, medicine, or mathematics do. It asks us to embark on a search which has not yet succeeded and, for all we know, may never succeed. The problem is that without a *claim* of success, the issue of whether there are any essenes, whether the search is legitimate, remains open. It is here that the subject matter of Socratic philosophy is related to its goal or end. Why embark on a search which may never be completed? How will it improve the quality of human life to try to formulate a theory which, owing to human limitations, is out of reach?

Interestingly enough, the image of philosophy as a conversation is not unique to Socrates. It has recently been invoked by Richard Rorty, a critic of essentialism and the whole attempt to measure social practices by adopting an epistemological stance which goes beyond them.[58] From Rorty's position, Socrates has put the philosopher in a

Sisyphean dilemma in which searching for definitions of the virtues is the most important thing a person can do even though we know, or have grounds to suspect, that the search is destined to fail.[54] The alternative is to reject the search for essence and the standards of rationality which motivate it. Why not adopt a notion of conversation according to which rationality is not beyond reach and explanations are not required to go beyond existing social practices but remain current with them?

This question, which asks Socrates to justify his way of life, is perfectly Socratic in spirit. Did he not ask similar questions of everyone else? If we take Socrates at his word about wanting to improve people's lives, the justification for his view of philosophy, including the search for essence and the dialectical conception of thought to which it gave rise, is to be found in the effect if had on the people to whom it was directed. Did Socrates have a positive effect on his jurors and respondets—not to mention his readers? Although he failed to find the moral theory he was searching for, did he also fail in his attempt to save souls? These are the questions we must ask.

Notes to Chapter Two

1. Richard Lewis Nettleship, *Lectures on Plato's Republic*, Second Edition (1901; rpt. New York: St. Martin's Press, 1967), 278–9.
2. See, for example, *Theaetetus* 189e and *Sophist* 263e. The precedent for this view of thinking is established at *Republic* 534b, where Socrates claims that a person who cannot give an account of the nature of each thing *either to himself or to another* is no dialectician. The passage implies that whether one is thinking to himself or answering another, the process is fundamentally the same: he must respond to objections or *elenchi* , 534c. Cf. 531e, 532d.
3. See *Meno* 75d and *Phaedrus* 276e. Cf. Xenophon, *Memorabilia* 4. 5. 11–12, where Socrates tries to work out an etymology.
4. Richard Robinson, *Plato's Earlier Dialectic*, Second Edition (London: Oxford University Press, 1953), 77. The main problem with Robinson's account of dialectic is his tendency to distinguish teaching and discovery. If Socrates stood for anything it was that *real* teaching can be nothing else. For further discussion, see my account of the slave-boy passage in Chapter Six.

5. Note that this passage is preceded by the claim that quickness of mind is not enough for philosophical discovery; one's soul must be "akin" to the nature of the object, by which Plato means that an unjust soul cannot have the illumination needed to grasp the nature of justice. This position will be treated in greater deatil below. For further discussion, see Glenn R. Morrow, *Plato's Epistles* (Indianapolis: Bobbs-Merrill, 1962), 75–81.

6. *Sophistical Refutations*, 169a37–62, 172a15–37.

7. See *Topics* 100a27–101a18 and, again, *Sophistical Refutations* 172a15–37. Aristotle does allow for the possibility that dialectic might be a prelude or propaedeutic to philosophical inquiry (*Topics* 101a36–b4). But I agree with Solmsen that his remarks in this passage are deceptive and should not be taken to mean that dialectic could rise above demonstrative reasoning as practiced by mathematicians. See "Dialectic without the Forms," in Owen (ed.), *Aristotle on Dialectic* (London: Oxford University Press, 1968), 24, n. 3. Needless to say, Plato argues in *Republic* VI-VII that dilectic is *superior* to mathematics because it gives an account of what each thing is (533b).

8. This conflicts with Xenophon's claim (*Memorabilia* 4.6.1b) that Socrates found *security* in commonly accepted opinions. Why, if he found such security in commonly accepted opinions, did he destroy so many of them? For further discussion, see Vlastos, "The Socratic Elenchus," ibid.

9. *Apology* 29d, 30a, 35c. Cf. *Gorgias* 454e.

10. Robinson, *op. cit.*, 15. But it is not true, as Robinson suggests on page 29, that these premises must *follow* from that thesis. This would put a severe restriction on the scope of elenctic inquiry. All that is required is that the respondent believe them so that if they are accepted, the original thesis cannot be.

11. See, for example, *Meno* 71d, *Charmides* 161c, *Statesman* 260b.

12. Robinson, *op. cit.*, 15.

13. Robinson, *op. cit.*, 80–4.

14. See *Gorgias* 448d–e, 463c, *Protagoras* 361c.

15. For a discussion of how the *Republic*'s view of dialectic is a continuation of Socrates' request for a definition, and how both are continued in later dialogues like the *Sophist* and *Statesman*, see Solmsen, *ibid*. Also see F. M. Cornford, "Mathematics and Dialectic in the *Republic* VI-VIII," in Allen (ed.), *Studies in Plato's Metaphysics* (New York: Humanities Press, 61–95. The problem with Cornford's account of dialectic is that he likens it to mathematical analysis. Even if Cornford is right about his view of analysis, this interpretation puts Plato in the position of borrowing from mathematics rather than criticizing it. For criticism of Cornford, see Cherniss, "Plato as Mathematician," *Review of Metaphysics* 4 (1950–51), 395–425 and Robinson, "Analysis in Greek Geometry," *Mind* n.s. 45 (1936), 464–73.

16. *Posterior Analytics* 92a34–b4: "How then is one who is defining something to prove its nature or essence? He will not do it by showing that if certain premises are true, something else necessarily follows, for that would be a demonstration; but neither will he show it as one who uses induction from a group of particular things when every particular exhibits a certain quality and there are no exceptions. For induction does not show what something is but that it has or fails to have an attribute." Cf. Gregory Vlastos, *"Anamnesis* in the *Meno," Dialogue* 4 (1965), 156: "Nor would there be any question of proving the *definitions* of this, or any other concept. We know how prominently definitions figure among the objects of Socratic search. But though Plato has said so far all too little of the methodology of the "What is it?" question, it is clear from what he says in the *Meno* itself, that he does not think that the true answer, when found, could be proved by deduction from the premises . . . " The reason for this is, as Vlastos sees, that if an answer to the "What is X?" question is prior to everything else we can know about X, there is nothing from which it can be deduced. The problem is that having made this point, Vlastos tries to explain recollection in terms of logical relations, meaning, and analyticity. But these concepts, which presuppose a sharp dichotomy between statements about meaning and statements about fact, have no precedent in the Socratic dialogues. The only way one could attribute a doctrine of analyticity to Socrates would be to assume that all truths not derived from the senses are analytic; in short, that *a priori* and analytic are the same thing. But where is the textual evidence for this assumption?

17. As Robinson point outs, *op. cit.* 46–8, Socrates did practise *epagoge*, which we might translate as "induction". But from Robinson's survey of the evidence, there is no reason to think that *epagogē* was a method for arriving at definitions.

18. Cf. Immanuel Kant, *Groundwork of the Metaphysic of Morals*, Paton trans. (New York: Harper and Row, 1948), 76: " . . . we cannot do Morality a worse service than by seeking to derive it from examples. Every sample of it presented to me must first itself be judged by moral principles in order to decide if it is fit to serve as an original example—that is, as a model: it can in no way supply the prime source for the concept of morality. Even the Holy One of the gospel must first be compared with our ideal of moral perfection before we can recognize him to be such." According to Gerasimos Santas, "The Socratic Fallacy," *Journal of the History of Philosophy* 10 (1974), 140, *Euthyphro* 6e tells us that appeal to a standard is only *one way* of deciding whether a particular thing exemplifies a given quality. But he never tells us what the alternatives are or where in the text Socrates recognizes them. For further discussion see M. F. Burnyeat "Examples in Epistemology: Socrates, Theaetetus, and G. E. Moore," *Philosophy* 52 (1977), 381–398.

19. R. E. Allen, *Plato's "Euthyphro" and the Earlier Theory of Forms* (New York: Humanities Press, 1970), 116.
20. For further discussion, see, once again, Burnyeat, *ibid.*
21. That is why Santas, *ibid.* is wrong to suggest that Socrates' search for definitions relies on induction. Socrates does ask Meno to say what is common to the various items he has enumerated (*Meno* 72c). But this cannot possibly mean that these items are thereby accepted as legitimate cases of virtue. The only reason Socrates asks Meno to say what is common to them is that he needs a general statement about virtue in order for the *elenchus* to proceed. But the general statement Meno proposes is soon rejected, and with it, the cases it was meant to justify.
22. *Peloponnesian War* 3.82, Warner trans.
23. On the revolutionary nature of Socratic *elenchus*, see *Gorgias* 481b–c: "Tell me, Socrates, are we to suppose now that you are serious or that you are having fun? For if you are serious, and what you say is actually true, wouldn't our lives as human beings be turned upside down and wouldn't it seem that everything we do is the opposite of what we ought to be doing?"
24. On this issue, see Irwin, *op. cit.*, 63. Where I disagree with Irwin is his contention (43) that Socrates wants a rule to project from easy examples of a disputed term to difficult ones. There are too many cases where "easy" examples are challenged, e.g., *Laches* 196e–197c.
25. P. T. Geach, "Plato's *Euthyphro*: An Analysis and Commentary," *The Monist* 50 (1966), 371.
26. John Rawls, *A Theory of Justice* (Cambridge, Harvard University Press, 1971), 20.
27. Kraut, *op. cit.*, 279–80. The reason the dialogues typically fall short in their attempts to define the virtues is that the discussions are not supported by insights in moral psychology. This is corrected in the *Republic* as Kraut (280) admits. For further discussion, see Henry Teloh, *The Developments of Plato's Metaphysics* (Univesity Park: The Pennsylvania State University Press, 1981), 34–5, 46.
28. Socrates' questions normally do not call for analytic statements but ordinary, first-order value judgments. Cf. Terence Irwin, *op. cit.*, 63–4. Terry Penner has argued that Socratic inquiry cannot be forced into the analytic/synthetic mold, see "The Unity of Virtue," *Philosophical Review* 82 (1973), 35–68. I agree completely. But Penner goes on to claim that the "What is it?" question is a request for a causal account. This cannot be right if *cause* in interpreted as the sort of thing investigated by modern empirical science. There are a lot of cases in the history of science when the effect is identified independently of the cause. But this is what Socrates appears to be ruling out at *Euthyphro* 6e and *Hippias Major* 286c–d when he argues that knowledge of the essence is needed to identify particular cases. Socrates' question is not "What causes the virtuous action

to occur?'' but "Why is the action which has occurred *virtuous?*'' In his reply to Penner, Vlastos defends the view that the "What is it?'' question is calling for "analysis of a concept.'' But he never tells us what he means by *analysis*, and in the current environment, it is difficult to say exactly what it involves. Vlastos offers Socrates' definition of quickness at *Laches* 192a–b as an example of the sort of thing Socrates is looking for in a definition. No doubt, this definition is an improvement on the kind of responses Laches had made up to that point. If Laches could come up with a definition with this degree of generality, the discussion would be greatly improved. Notice, however, that *quickness* is not a disputed term. It is therefore presuming too much to think that Socrates would be satisfied by an equally brief account of courage. To solve the kinds of disputes which pertain to courage, we would have to go beyond anything appropriately termed *analysis* and propose a theory of how people respond to fear, what fears are justifiable, etc. See "What did Socrates Understand by His 'What is F?' Question,'' in *Platonic Studies*, Second Edition (Princeton: Princeton University Press, 1981), 410–417.

29. Perhaps that is what Xenophon meant when he said that Socrates began with commonly accepted beliefs (see no. 8 above). It may be objected that in the discussion with Meno's slave, Socrates launches into an esoteric subject. The answer is, I think, that he is questioning the boy about spatial relationships which are intuitively clear. Notice, for example, that the boy has no hesitation offering an opinion at the beginning of the inquiry. He does not experience dialectical paralysis until 84a, well into the discussion and has no trouble understanding the solution once Socrates provides the necessary hint.

30. In logic, an indirect argument normally goes as follows. To establish the truth of P, assume not-P and derive a contradiction. Since not-P is known to be false, it follows that P must be true. In Socratic *elenchus*, the usual form of argument is the reverse. The respondent asserts P. Show that P itself leads to a contradiction or is inconsistent with something else the respondent wants to assert. Therefore P is false. Rather than asserting the truth of not-P, Socrates asks the respondent to offer another definition Q. This assumes that definitions must be positive rather than negative.

31. Cf. Irwin, *Plato: Gorgias, op. cit.*, 181.

32. See Karl Popper, "Back to the Presocratics,'' in Allen (ed.), *op. cit.*, 153.

33. Irwin, *Plato's Moral Theory, op. cit.*, 70.

34. Cf. Vlastos' Assumption A in "The Socratic Elenchus,'' *ibid.*: Everyone's moral beliefs always include a subset of true beliefs which entail the negation of each of his false moral beliefs. According to Vlastos, this is a methodological assumption which is justified by experience: whenever Socrates encounters people who seem to have false beliefs, questioning can elicit true beliefs which are inconsistent with the false ones. But I

agree with Kraut that Vlastos' interpretation of this assumption is too strong. It does not mean that no matter how many revisions a person makes, he will always be forced to admit an inconsistency if he disagrees with the conclusions of Socratic morality. It may be logically possible for someone to maintain a consistent immoralism if he is willing to accept a number of unorthodox or implausible premises. The assumption which underlies Socratic *elenchus* is that in fact no one *will* accept such premises because everyone has enough moral knowledge to find them objectionable. So while it may be possible to identify premises which would entail the conclusions Callicles wants, not even Callicles could stomach them.

35. Vlastos, "The Socratic Elenchus," *op. cit.*, 27–8.

36. This difference is this. *Meno* 87b–c indicates that "Virtue can be taught" and "Virtue is a kind of knowledge" are convertible propositions; one implies the other. But while "Virtue is good" implies "Virtue is a kind of knowledge," there is nothing to indicate that the latter also implies the former. The lack of convertibility is what enabled Robinson to claim that the method employed in this passage is not mathematical analysis. Robinson, *op. cit.*, 114–122.

37. See, for example, Normal Gulley, *Plato's Theory of Knowledge* (London: Methuen, 1962), 14–5. According to Gulley, the method of hypothesis is to be understood in light of 97d–98e, where Socrates demands a chain of causal reasoning to convert true belief into knowledge. But everything in this chain follows from an *un*examined hypothesis: virtue is good, where "good' means "beneficial." How, then, can it constitute knowledge?

38. This point is made again at the end of the end of the dialogue (100b). It would appear, therefore, that Plato is holding up geometry as an example of a discipline which reverses the natural order of priority by putting a derivative question first. For a similar interpretation of the slave-boy passage, see Malcolm Brown, "Plato Disapproves of the Slave-Boy's Answer," in Brown (ed.) *Plato's Meno* (New York: Bobbs-Merrill, 1971), 198–242. For an opposing view, see J. T. Bedu-Addo, "Recollection and the Argument 'From a Hypothesis' in Plato's *Meno*," *Journal of Hellenic Studies* 104 (1984), 1–14. According to Bedu-Addo, the search for the essence of virtue is not abandoned when the method of hypothesis is introduced. But notice that to sustain this interpretation, he must argue that much of the dialogue, including the argument against the teaching of virtue, is not to be taken at face value. For a more detailed criticism of Bedu-Addo and discussion of the method of hypothesis, see my article "*Meno* 86c–89a: A Mathematical Image of Philosophic Inquiry," to appear in an upcoming *Festschrift* for Robert S. Brumbaugh edited by Brian Hendley.

39. See *Republic* 510b ff. and 533b–c: "For if your premise is something you do not know, and your conclusion and the intermediate steps a tangle of things you do not know, how could any conclusion you agree to ever

become knowledge?'' Cf. *Cratylus* 436d. Notice too, that the geometry problem used to illustrate the method uses the technique of application of areas, which is criticized at *Republic* 527a.

40. The first problem is whether the hypotheses Socrates is talking about could include definitions. According to Robinson, *op. cit.*, 136–7, the answer is no. Cf. Sayre, *op. cit.*, 28–30. The passage does not draw a clear distinction between (a) a statement of essence (what is Beauty?), (b) a statement of existence (Beauty exists), and (c) a statement of causality (beautiful things are such because they partake in the form of Beauty). I would argue that the hypotheses do not exclude definitions but neither are they limited to them. If definitions are excluded, it is hard to see how the passage could be autobiographical, which it is clearly meant to be. On the other hand, since the passage concerns the issue of causality, a definition alone could not suffice: it would have to be supported by metaphysical assumptions. The second problem is how to interpret ''accord.'' Does this mean ''follows from'' or ''is consistent with.'' For a review of the available opinions, see Robinson, *op. cit.*, 129–36, and David Gallop, *Plato: Phaedo* (Oxford: Clarendon Press ,1975), 179–81. I am in basic agreement with Gallop that neither deducibility nor bare logical consistency are adequate descriptions of what Socrates has in mind. The mere fact that a statement is consistent with a theory is hardly grounds for claiming that the statement is true. On the other hand, it is doubtful that the explanation the theory of forms is supposed to provide is strictly logical. Participation in the form of Beauty may explain why a rose is beautiful even though the beauty of the rose does not follow as a *logical* consequence of the theory. The relation between a theory and its applications is neither as loose as consistency nor as strict as deducibility. The problem is that Socrates glosses over these issues by using the metaphor of accord.

41. ''Virtue is good'' is called an hypothesis at *Meno* 87d. According to Robinson, *op. cit.*, 93–133, an hypothesis in Plato is first and foremost a proposition put forward in order to prove something else, not a proposition put forward in order to be itself tested.

42. See *Republic* 533b–c, quoted above in no. 37 and cf. Frege, *The Foundation of Arithmetic*, Second Edition, translated by J. L. Austin (Oxford: Clarendon, 1959), ix.

43. Cornford, *op. cit.*, 86. where I disagree with Cornford is his claim that there is a separate method for mathematical and moral dialectic. I do not see how such a distinction is implied at 534b–d nor why the reference to forms (*eidē*) of dialectic at 532d indicates that there has to be such a sharp dichotomy. Notice that much of Cornford's evidence comes from sources external to the *Republic*, e.g., Aristotle, Sextus and Plato's *Parmenides*.

44. Robinson, *op. cit.*, 172–3.

45. Compare Popper, '' . . . There is no such thing as a logical method of

having new ideas, or a logical reconstruction of this process," *The Logic of Scientific Discovery* (London: Hutchinson, 1959), 32.

46. 344a-b.

47. See, for example, *Phaedo* 80d, 81a, *Republic* 486d, 487a, 501d. Cf. *Phaedo* 67b and 82c, where Socrates claims it is against nature for what is impure to come into contact with what is pure, *Republic* 500c-d, where he claims that the philosopher will become like the forms he is contemplating and *Phaedrus* 250b-c, where the similarity between knower and object known is stressed repeatedly.

48. Robinson, *op. cit.*, 174. Robinson's interpretation is criticized by Kenneth Sayre in *Plato's Analytic Method* (Chicago: University of Chicago Press, 1969), 51-6. Sayre's point is that it does nothing to claim that the upward path of dialectic culminates in a final intuition. Reference to intuition does not answer the question of what the upward path consists in, it only restates it: what kind of intuition and how is it achieved? According to Sayre, Plato was moving towards the method of collection and division described in the *Theaetetus* and *Sophist*. Perhaps, but even Sayre admits that as far as the *Republic* is concerned, Plato was still unclear on what the upward path was. For further discussion, also see Julius A. Elias, *Plato's Defense of Poetry* (Albany: SUNY Press, 1984), Chapter Two. I agree with Elias about the inconclusiveness of dialectic but not about the status of poetry.

49. *Laches* 192c and *Charmides* 159c-d. This assumption is what enables Socrates to reject definitions of the virtues which identify them with morally neutral traits like endurance or quietness.

50. Cf. Kraut, *op. cit.*, 245-67. I will suggest in a later chapter that by the end of his life, Socrates put forward what we might call a second order conception of virtue; that is, a conception of virtue which takes into consideration the fact that human knowlege is too limited to discover the complete moral theory he has been searching for.

51. Compare Normal Gulley, *The Philosophy of Socrates* (London: Macmillan, 1968), 69: "Socrates might be professing ignorance merely as an expedient to encourage his interlocutor to seek out the truth, to make him think that he is joining with Socrates in a voyage of discovery." But Socrates explicitly denies this at *Apology* 23a, where there would be no point in continuing the "pretense" of ignorance. Again, lack of a moral theory does not entail lack of moral conviction.

52. Notice that the definitions of the virtues advanced in *Republic IV* are part of a much wider theory about social organization and the composition of the human soul.

53. Richard Rorty, *Philosophy and the Mirror of Nature* (Princeton: Princeton University Press, 1970), 389-394.

54. Rorty, *op. cit.*, 374.

Chapter Three
Socrates as Speech Maker

DESPITE EVERYTHING WHICH HAS been said about dialogue, one text comes as close to being a monologue as anything could: the *Apology*. There is a small section in which Socrates cross examines Meletus, but it is not terribly important, and the great bulk of the piece is Socrates addressing the jury. Socrates admits at the outset that he is uncomfortable with this situation and would prefer to do things in the usual way. Still, the *Apology* is not a dialogue in the normal sense of the term and that raises questions about its appeal. Is it an inferior piece of work? Does it lack the philosophical profundity of Plato's other writings? I believe that the answer to these questions is no but to see this we will have to ask what the *Apology* is trying to do.

To begin with, the *Apology* is a masterpiece of forensic oratory. Within a short time of Socrates' death, it was imitated by no less a stylist than Isocrates.[1] In his notes on the text, John Burnet pointed out that Socrates' speech also could be read as parody. He concluded that'' . . . just as in the *Phaedrus* Socrates improves on the current rhetorical commonplaces by giving them a deeper meaning . . . ''[2] There are, of course, passages where he appears to be using such commonplaces to his own advantage. In this connection, one thinks of his challenge to Meletus to produce witnesses against him or his willingness to die rather than beg the jury for his life.

The parody thesis was attacked by Hackforth on the ground that Socrates claims at the beginning (17b) that he is not a clever speaker.[3] If he is not a clever speaker, how can we expect him to produce an artful parody of those who are? If he is a clever speaker, then he has begun his defense with a palpable falsehood. But this argument overlooks one point: a disclaimer about speaking ability is itself a rhetorical commonplace.[4] Instead of contradicting the parody thesis, this remark may in fact support it.

Rather than discuss these points in the abstract, I wish to compare Plato's *Apology* with a particular piece of Greek oratory: Gorgias' *Apology of Palamedes*. My examination will show that the *Apology of Socrates* is not only a parody of existing commonplaces, but a parody which takes Gorgias' speech as its prime example. My reasons for making this claim are two: (1) there are a surprising number of similarities between the two speeches—more than can be accounted for by coincidence, and (2) viewing the *Apology of Socrates* as a parody allows us to see important connections between it and Plato's discussion of rhetoric in the *Gorgias*. It is thus significant that when Socrates is forced to deliver a monologue, he calls attention to the differences between himself and a man who made monologues his life's work.

The first person to point out the verbal similarities between the *Apology of Scorates* and the *Apology of Palamedes* was Heinrich Gomperz.[5] But all Gomperz wanted to establish was the authenticity of the latter. Kathleen Freeman remarked on the ''striking resemblances'' between the two orations but went no further.[6] In 1957, Guido Calogero maintained that the *Apology of Socrates* is a record of Socrates' debt to Gorgias.[7] Yet most scholars regard Calogero's view as fanciful. A more plausible suggestion is that by comparing Socrates to Palamedes, Plato is providing Socrates' speech with a mythological background.[8] The most comprehensive study of the two speeches is a monograph written by James Coulter in 1964.[9] Coulter contends that the Palamedes sets forth a view of rhetoric which the *Apology of Socrates* explicitly rejects. But he does not mention the parody thesis, and therefore misses what may be the most important point.

1. RHETORIC AS AN APPEAL TO PROBABILITY

According to legend, Palamedes was noted for ingenuity. He is credited with the invention of the alphabet, the systematization of weights and measures, and numerous helpful devices. When Odysseus feigned madness to escape going to war, it was Palamedes who called his bluff by putting the baby Telemachos on the ground in front of the plow. In the early part of the Trojan War, Odysseus was sent on an expedition to bring back a supply of grain. When he returned empty handed, Palamedes ridiculed him. Odysseus claimed that Palamedes could do no better, whereupon Palamedes returned with a full supply. Odysseus then devised a plot to make Palamedes look like a traitor. A pot of gold was buried in Palamedes' tent and a prisoner was forced to deliver a letter which seemed to implicate Palamedes in treason. The plot succeeded, and Palamedes, falsely accused, was stoned to death.

Gorgias' supposed defense of Palamedes reads like a set speech which students were asked to memorize and imitate. Imitation would not be difficult because the speech is so devised that nearly anyone on trial could plug in the details of his own case. In outline, it has all the parts of a standard, forensic address: (1) an introduction in which the speaker apologizes for lack of speaking ability, (2) a narration in which he recounts the events which led up to the trial, (3) a disposition in which he formally denies the charges against him, and (4) and epilogue in which he asks the jury to take its duties seriously.

Although the *Palamedes* strikes us as a ponderous speech, its basic line of argument became so widespread that it is possible to view it as a paradigm of sophistical oratory. Again and again, the speaker tries to show that it would be implausible to suppose that anyone in his position did what he is accused of doing. How could I? Why would I?—and so on for paragraph after paragraph. In the antithetical style for which Gorgias became famous, he tells us: "I could not wish to attempt such deeds, if I had the power, nor could I have the power, if I wished."[10] At another point, he argues that no one could have committed this crime for any of the usual motives. He then sums up: "Wouldn't my life have been unlivable if I had done these things?" The jury is supposed to decide that it would have been and conclude that Palamedes therefore did not do them.

The crux of this speech is its appeal to probability. Rather than look to the facts, the jury is asked to weight the chances that something might have happened in the circumstances described by the speaker. Not surprisingly, in the *Phaderus* (267a), Plato "credits" Gorgias and his teacher Tisias with the realization that probabilities (*ta eikota*) deserve higher esteem than truth. In other words, they have discovered that the facts of a case may have little to do with deciding its outcome. As Socrates tells us in an earlier passage (*Phaedrus* 272d–e):

> . . . he who is to become a competent speaker need not bother with the truth about just or good behavior . . . For in the courts nobody has any concern for the truth about these things: their only concern is with the plausible. And this is identical with the probable so that whoever is going to master the art of speaking

must devote his attention to probability. On some occasions, one should not even say what actually happened, if its occurrence was improbable, but go into court armed with probabilities, whether for the prosecution or the defense . . .

Along these lines, Plato claims that Tisias once argued that if a weak but brave man assaulted a strong but cowardly one, neither should go into court stating the truth. Instead the coward should say that the weak man did not act alone, and the brave man should ask a question along the lines of: How could a little person like me possibly attack a big one like him?[11]

The fault of this sort of argument is easy to detect. As Aristotle (*Rhet.* 1402a12–13) once said, the improbable sometimes happens; therefore it is probablle that improbable events will occur. Nor is it difficult to see how this observation could become a powerful weapon in the hands of a smooth and quick witted speaker. Depending on his strategy, almost anything could be shown to be probable, or improbable, or both. A lively imagination is all that is needed to portray normal events in a strange light or strange events in a normal one.[12]

It is clear, however, that the orator who argues from probability is seeking to persuade his audience without really educating them—precisely what Gorgias describes himself as doing in the dialogue bearing his name (454e–455a). When he asks them to consider the probability that something might happen, he is not providing new information but inviting them to decide the case on the basis of the prejudices they already have. To establish a fact, one has to present evidence; but to establish probability, he need only tell a story or crack a joke. Thus rhetorical dexterity is extremely important to one who uses this argument. A good orator can persuade his audience with no knowledge of what actually happened. This more than anything else is the lesson of Gorgias' speech.

2. BEATING THE RHETORICIANS AT THEIR OWN GAME

To return to the *Apology of Socrates*, the speaker begins his defense in the usual way: he must be excused for not being a gifted orator. But Socrates' words belie him since his ability as a speaker is well documented in the rest of the Platonic corpus. It is praised by Gorgias (455d), Protagoras (361d), and Phaedrus (257c); in the latter case, it is compared favorably to that of Lysias, one of the most successful speech writers of the day. Burnet has shown that the *Apology* too has all the parts of a standard, forensic address, and we have seen that it served as a model for Isocrates.

Most commentators attribute Socrates' disclaimer to irony; but in this case, it is worth noting that the irony is not his. He has borrowed a stock device which was used by speakers before him and can be found in court rooms even today. In fact, Gorgias' Palamedes said practically the same thing, and Socrates' words read like a paraphrase of his: "I am at a loss to know what to say unless I learn something from the truth . . . "[13]

Nor is this the only device Socrates has "borrowed." For example, each speaker uses his modest financial condition as a sign of sincerity (*Pal.* 15; *Apol.* 31c), indicating that jurors are likely to resent someone richer than they. Each challenges the accuser to produce witnesses against him knowing perfectly well that none can be found (*Pal.* 22; *Apol.* 33c–34a). Each claims the charges against him are not only false but contradictory (*Pal.* 25–26; *Apol.* 34c ff.). Each argues that not only is he innocent, he is a benefactor to those who sit in judgment upon him (*Pal.* 30; *Apol.* 36d). Each makes the standard gesture of rejecting appeals to pity or favors from friends (*Pal.* 33; *Apol.* 35c, 38e–39b). Each finds death preferable to dishonor—and at practically the same place in the speech (*Pal.* 35; *Apol.* 28b–d, 38d–39b).

The instructions to the jury proceed in a similar fashion. Each speaker asks it not to rush in deciding the case and not to hurry what nature herself will accomplish in due time (*Pal.* 34–35; *Apol.* 37a–b, 39c). Each asks it to pay more attention to actions (*erga*) than it does to words (*logoi*), even though neither speaker has any difficulty expressing himself (*Pal.* 34; *Apol.* 32a). Each warns the jury it will lose face by condemning an innocent man (*Pal.* 36; *Apol.* 38c). Each attempts to establish his innocence by invoking the "Socratic Paradox" that no one willingly does evil (*Pal.* 13–14; *Apol.* 25d–e). As if this is not enough, Socrates compares himself to Palamedes at *Apology* 41b.

The point in calling attention to these similarities is not to argue that the *Apology of Socrates* owes its persuasiveness to Gorgias. Unlike the *Apology of Socrates*, Gorgias' *Palamedes* is not a masterpiece of world literature; it is a collection of *topoi*—tried and true devices for winning acquittal. Rather, the point is that despite his disclaimer, Socrates' speech is no amateur performance. On the contrary, he knew all the tricks of the trade and employed them with consummate skill.

In one respect, what has happened is quite remarkable. A poor man unaccustomed to speaking in public, gets up and delivers a speech which surpasses the best efforts of professionals. There is, of course, a simple explanation for this. The author of the *Apology* is not Socrates but Plato. It is not, therefore, the work of a poor man unfamiliar with appropriate court room demeanor. Writing forensic speeches on behalf of historical figures was a literary genre all its own. No doubt Plato wished to portray Socrates in the best possible light. One way to do this was to have him beating the rhetoricians at their own game. But we cannot conclude that the historical Socrates was as articulate as Plato suggests. There is even a tradition which holds that Socrates said nothing at all.[14]

The question of whether the *Apology* is Socrates' speech or Plato's literary creation is one of those scholarly debates which is no closer to being resolved today than it was a hundred years ago. Plato was not bound by the standards of modern historians and may have followed Thucydides in staying as close as possible to the sense of what the speaker said but supplementing it by "what was demanded of the speaker by the occasion."[15] Most scholars would agree that the greater the artistic merit of the *Apology*, the less the likelihood that it is faithful to Socrates' actual defense. Could a person untrained in public speaking step before a court and deliver a subtly constructed parody of a well known rhetorical paradigm? Ordinarily the answer would be no, but we must keep in mind that Socrates was no ordinary person. The only thing we have a right to claim is that Plato is the author and that he did, in fact, produce a rhetorical masterpiece. The question of historical accuracy simply cannot be answered. In everything which follows, I will treat the *Apology* as Plato's creation— not because there is independent evidence of what Socrates said but because in the absence of such evidence, this is the most reasonable assumption. On the other hand, it is true, as Burnet suggests, that if Plato wrote an idealized version of the original speech, it could not be too far from the real thing since there were at least 501 other witnesses. A completely fanciful version surely would have aroused a protest.[16]

All questions of historical accuracy aside, one must account for the coherence of the *Apology* as a work of literature. We still have a rhetorical masterpiece supposedly given by a man who claims he has no talent as a speaker. The masterpiece not only imitates a well-known model, it improves on it. There is, then, a seeming incongruity in Plato's portrait. Socrates' accusers warned the jury he would try to win them over with rhetorical splendor (17a–b). If so, then Plato shows him playing right into their hands. To paraphrase R. E. Allen, in circumstances which call for appearing as an ordinary, domesticated farmyard fowl, Plato has given Socrates the character of a fox.[17] Worse, he has not shown Socrates beating the rhetoricians at their own game. Whatever its accomplishments from an aesthetic standpoint, the *Apology of Socrates* is a failure from a practical one: the speaker does not convince the jury of his innocence.

3. RHETORIC AND MORAL IMPROVEMENT

To understand the dramatic context of the *Apology*, we must consider Plato's discussion of rhetoric in the *Gorgias*. Certainly it would be to his advantage for us to see that the same rhetorical devices can be found on the lips of a Gorgias, a Socrates, a Callicles, or anyone wishing to persuade an audience of anything. Since the purpose of rhetoric, as defined by Gorgias, is merely to induce belief (454e), there are no limitations on who can use it or for what purpose. Rhetoric, in other words, is indifferent to truth or falsity, innocence or guilt. Once mastered, it will work as well for the demagogue as it does for the statesman.

But as Allen has shown, Socrates has two conceptions of persuasion. The first induces belief (*peitho pisteutikē*), while the second provides instruction (*peitho didaskalikē*).[18] To each type of persuasion, there corresponds a type of rhetoric: one is a species of flattery which aims at gratification, the other has the same aim as Socratic philosophy: improving the soul. Yet it is impossible to tell them apart on the basis of technique alone. Common rhetoric may lack nothing in the way of polish. One has only to read the speeches of Thucydides' *History* to see that this is so. Nor can one tell them apart on the basis of their stated goals. Flattery succeeds only to the extent it can pass itself off as something better.

Common rhetoric, like faulty sense perception, does not wear its true colors on its sleeve. Thus Plato's distinction gives rise to a problem. If Socrates and Gorgias employ the same rhetorical devices in their respective apologies, how is one to know to what she is listening—a sincere account of a man's life or a verbal *tour de force*? The charges agains Socrates (19b–c) indicate that he was perceived as a sophist. Like Gorgias, he had no mastery of a legitimate art such as medicine, architecture, or military strategy; he spent most of his waking hours talking. During the reign of the Thirty Tyrants, Critias, his former associate, took revenge on him by forbidding anyone to teach an art of discourse—precisely what Gorgias describes himself as doing in Plato's dialogue.[19] We have seen that in the *Apology*, Plato has

Socrates identify his life's work as a kind of persuasion (30a). Yet despite these outward similarities, Socrates and Gorgias were as different as night and day. To borrow an analogy Plato uses in the *Sophist* (231a), the dog and the wolf may resemble one another if seen from afar, but one is the tamest of animals, the other the fiercest.

Still, the question remains: How is one to know to what she is listening? It will not do to say that the jury should have been able to see that Socrates was sincere and let the matter drop. Somewhere in the *Apology of Socrates* there ought to be a clue which allows one to distinguish his defense from the "standard" defense composed by Gorgias.

That clue is found at 17b, when Socrates maintains that he is a clever speaker *if* by that expression one means a speaker who tells the truth. Though Gorgias' Palamedes made essentially the same claim, we have seen that he was concerned less with truth than with probability. It is here that Socrates' defense departs from Palamedes'. For if Plato had imitated Gorgias to the letter, he would have written a defense of Socrates which made ample use of the argument from probability.[20] The outlines of such a defense are not difficult to imagine. All one has to do is paraphrase Callicles' warning to Socrates in the *Gorgias* (486a ff.):

> A person who spends his time discussing philosophy would
> not be able to defend himself if brought into court on
> trumped up charges. Do you think, gentlemen, that knowing
> this I would have gone around Athens flaunting disrespect for
> the gods? Far from it. A person as inept at public speaking as
> I am must be extremely cautious in such matters. He must see
> to it that all his actions are just and noble so as not to run the
> risk of aiding his enemies. Therefore the charges against me
> are an insult to common sense. No reasonable person in my
> circumstances would dare be impious.

Perhaps this is what Socrates should have said, but it is hardly how the text of the *Apology* reads. In cross-examining Meletus, Socrates reminded the jurors of why he was considered a verbal wizard and thereby reinforced the prejudices against him. He insulted the politicians, poets, and artisans in the jury by claiming that when it came to justice and piety, none of them knew what he was talking about. Worse, he realized that in one respect he was a clever speaker and said so without hesitation. Again, following Burnet, he employed Gorgias' techniques but did so not to establish the probability of his innocence but the truth about his life.[21] Truth, it may be said, is something of which Gorgias was wary. In the *Helen*, he maintained that a speech delights and persuades (*eterpse kai epeise*) a large audience by the skill with which it is written, not by the truth of what it says (13). More important, in the *Palamedes*, he described truth as one of the "teachers more dangerous than resourceful" (4).

If truth is a dangerous ally for a public speaker, then Socrates took a great risk in speaking the way he did. True rhetoric does not attempt to flatter the jury but to educate it. In fact, its aim is stated by Socrates in a part of the *Apology* which is almost certainly a reply to *Gorgias*: not to delight and persuade but to educate and persuade (*didaskein kai peithein*, 35c). Thus the best sign of Socrates' sincerity was not the delight his speech produced but the irritation: "I know quite well that this is why I have become hated—which is also proof that what I am saying is true" (24a). Warm feelings toward the accused are the sort of thing which ought to make the jury think twice about its verdict because they are the most immediate effects of common rhetoric. The Socrates of the *Apology* did not arouse them (cf. 30c). As a result, the jury became angry and voted to convict.

But despite its outcome, the *Apology* is coherent. Socrates claims he is not a clever speaker in the sense in which his accusers intended. Nothing in the dialogue contradicts this. If the purpose of forensic oratory is to win acquittal, then Socrates has no talent as a forensic speaker. Not only is he convicted, he is sentenced to death. Given the closeness of the vote (36a), there is reason to think that a speech containing fewer taunts and insults might have produced a different result. So it is not true that Socrates failed to beat the rhetoricians at their own game; rather, he refused to play it. His mastery of Gorgias' techniques indicates he could have given a standard, forensic speech if he had wanted. In fact, he says as much in a passage which can be read as a reply to Callicles' charge that a philosopher cannot defend himself in court (*Gorg.* 486a–b): "Perhaps you believe, gentlemen, that I have been convicted for lack of words to persuade you, if I had thought it proper to do or say anything to gain an acquittal. Far from it. It is true I have been convicted for a lack, not of words, but of boldness and shamelessness—unwillingness to say to you the sort of things it would please you to hear" (*Apology* 38d).

The reason Socrates did not give the standard, forensic speech is, in his words, that it is unworthy of a free man (38e). Once again, his words are echoed in the *Gorgias*. Freedom (*eleutheria*, 452d) is what Gorgias promised his students if they studied rhetoric. Yet, according to Socrates, the typical forensic speaker is a slave both to the time clock and the desires of the audience (cf. *Theaetetus* 172b ff.). It is for this reason that the Socrates of the *Gorgias* describes rhetoric as a kind of flattery (*kolakeia*, 463b). The connotations of this word are extremely low. As E. R. Dodds put it: "The *kolax* is what the eighteenth century called a toad-eater or lickspittle and schoolboys call a bumsucker."[22] While common rhetoric may promise freedom, it depends for its effectiveness on the most shameless sort of degradation.

True rhetoric offers freedom—but at a price. It takes as its guiding principle that success or failure is not determined by the vote of a jury. Thus after learning of his conviction, Socrates expresses no regrets about the manner of his defense (38e). Rather, the purpose of true rhetoric is to seek the moral improvement of the audience. But true rhetoric cannot, for that reason, dispense with aesthetic considerations. On the contrary, it must pay more attention to them than base rhetoric does. As Socrates tells us in the *Gorgias* (503d–504a).

> Come then, the good man who pays heed to the best when he speaks, will not say what he does at random but with an eye to something. Just as the other craftsmen, with an eye to their proper function, apply the measure they do, not at random, but in order to give some from to the thing on which they are working. Look, if you wish, at painters, builders, shipwrights, and all the other craftsmen, whichever you like, to see how each of them arranges everything on which he is working according to some order and forces one part to fit and suit another, until the whole thing has been put together to make an orderly and systematic whole.

In short, Socrates' eloquence is not incongruous. It follows from his desire to speak the truth. He is a clever speaker in the sense in which *he* intended, and nothing in the dialogue contradicts this either.

4. THE PURPOSE OF PARODY

To show that the *Apology* is coherent is not, however, to show that it is a parody. To establish the latter, one must show what Plato was trying to accomplish by writing a parody and why he wrote it the way he did. The first thing to notice, in this regard, is that Gorgias too had taken to writing parodies. From what we can tell, his essay *On Nature of the Non-Existent* attempted to "prove" three things: (1) that nothing exists, (2) that even if something did exist, we could not have any knowledge of it, and (3) that even if we did have knowledge of it, we could not communicate it. Although some have interpreted this text as a serious treatise in metaphysics and epistemology, the silliness of its conclusions, let alone the shoddiness of its inferences, argue otherwise.[23] What Gorgias appears to have done is to construct a parody of the abstract and often bizarre reasoning of the Eleatic philosophers. He takes arguments whose purpose is to lead to truth and directs them instead to palpable falsehoods. The reader is supposed to conclude jthat such arguments can be used to prove anything and therefore it is foolish to put much stock in them.

If the sophists could parody their opponents, so too could Plato. In the *Phaedrus*, he makes fun of the speeches of Lysias. In the *Protagoras*, he makes fun of the whole enterprise of literary analysis. After the discussion between Socrates and Protagoras breaks down at 334c, it is agreed that Protagoras will ask the questions and Socrates answer. Protagoras resumes the discussion by asking Socrates to consider a poem by Simonides. But when Protagoras is finished, Socrates takes over and gives the audience a lesson in textual criticism it will never forget. He portrays Sparta as a center of learning and Simonides as a philosopher of considerable subtlety. In fact, so subtle is Simonides' philosophy that it bears a striking resemblance to Socrates' own! There is a sharp distinction between being and becoming (344a), a close comparison between being good and being wise (344e–345c), and a commitment to the Socratic dictum that no one willing does evil (345d–e). Throughout Socrates' "interpretation" of the poem, words are moved around, important passages ignored, support derived from extraneous sources, and, in general, no attention paid to the author's own intentions.[24]

Socrates' parody of literary analysis is meant as a criticism of Protagoras. Explicating poetry is a dubious way of teaching virtue because, as Socrates' exercise makes clear, a little ingenuity is all that is needed to put the most astonishing doctrines in someone else's mouth. To the extent that Protagoras used such methods, his teaching was a sham.

To return to the *Apology*, we have, once again, an obvious disparity between method and purpose. Socrates employs Gorgias' devices but does so to accomplish something Gorgias never intended. As Jacqueline de Romilly once said, Gorgias argued in the *Helen* that the essence of rhetoric is to deceive—that it is *apatē*.[25] But rather than flat-

ter the jury and obscure the truth, Socrates uses these devices to ir-
ritate the jury and make truth the focal point of his address. Tools
designed for a particular purpose are put to work to do the opposite.
In effect, Socrates has turned Gorgias on his head.

The conclusion is that, like Protagoras' way of teaching virtue,
Gorgias' tools are a sham. Anyone can stand before a jury and imitate
a set speech with stock devices—even a person unaccustomed to
speaking in public. But not everyone is innocent of the charges
brought against him. Thus the fact that someone uses these devices
proves nothing. What matters is that the jury be able to look beyond
rhetorical niceties to the issue of innocence or guilt (35c–d). As Burnet
put it: "We have the usual *topoi* indeed, but they are all made to lead
up to the genuinely Socratic paradox that the function of a good
orator is to tell the truth."[26]

The audience's reaction to this paradox must have been puzzle-
ment (cf. *Crito* 46e). Despite the mandatory proclamations, truth is
the last thing one expects from a forensic speaker. One can imagine
someone in the audience saying something fairly close to the question
Callicles poses in the *Gorgias* (481b): Tell me, Socrates, are you
serious? Socrates is the speaker who typically gives one the opposite
of what he expects. In so doing, he has borrowed another of Gorgias'
devices: to meet your opponent's earnestness with levity and his levity
with earnestness.[27] He scoffs at the threat of death (28b–d, 30b) and
proposes a ludicrous penalty after the verdict has been announced
(36d–e). But this does not mean that he trifles with the real subject of
his defense: justice and piety. According to Socrates, the person who
trifles with such things is Meletus (24c).

But parodies succeed only if the audience is aware that what it is
hearing is, in face, a parody. In Socrates' case, this was not so. Undoubtedly the jury did become suspicious of the standard, forensic
devices but failed to see, as Burnet put it, that Socrates had given
them a deeper meaning. If nothing else, the *Apology* is proof that such
devices are not infallible. *This* time the jury decided it was not going
to be charmed by a verbal wizard and voted to convict. In one respect,
the verdict was correct: the normal forensic rhetoric practised in
courts does have a corrupting influence on the young. The tragedy of
the *Apology* is that the jury was unable to determine who was using it
and sentenced the wrong man.

5. A BENEFACTOR TO THE CITY?

E. R. Dodds once described the impression created by Gorgias' work as that of a "dazzling insincerity."[28] But Dodds' opinion could not have been shared by the average fifth-century Greek. A person does not become rich, famous, and widely imitated by convincing people he does not mean what he says. The dazzling insincerity would be a better description of the audience's reaction to Socrates. As Allen suggests, the *Apology* presents us with an elaborate case of mistaken identity—a case of confusing true rhetoric with common, the substance with its shadow.[29] In the *Gorgias* (464c–d), Plato reflects on this fact by pointing out that common rhetoric is an imposter, It offers pleasure as a substitute for goodness and probability as a substitute for thuth.

But common rhetoric has an appeal which, in Socrates' words, is almost supernatural (*Gorgias* 456a). Gorgias argued that through a kind of witchcraft, it can actually change the soul of the listener (*Helen*, 13–14). To return to the language of the *Sophist*, it can cast a magical spell which makes a wolf appear like a dog and gets the dog to take the punishment intended for the wolf. In this connection, it is interesting to note what happened when Gorgias addressed the Athenian Assembly in 427 B.C. The first-century historian Diodorus Siculus tells us: "When he arrived in Athens and was brought before the people, he spoke to them about the alliance and, by the novelty of his speech, he amazed the Athenians, who are cultivated people and fond of discourse. For he was the first to make use of extraordinary and carefully planned sentence structures such as those involving antithesis, balance, clauses of equal length and similar endings, as well as other such devices. . ." (Diels and Krantz, 82. A. 4). Again from Gorgias, a speech delights and persuades an audience by the skill with which it is written.

The overall theme of the *Apology* is to present Socrates in the tragic light of someone who wants to help the city but is spurned by it. This establishes the link with Palamedes. Faced with a choice between the dog and the wolf, the city picks the wolf. References to this tragedy occur in the *Gorgias* (521e–522), *Phaedo* (63b), *Republic* (487b–497a), and *Theaetetus* (172b–177c); it is, therefore, one of the most consistent themes in the Platonic corpus. If the philosopher seeks to go *behind* popular opinion and current social practises, it is because left to its own devices, the city has erred disastrously. If Socrates is right, it cannot even identify its own benefactor (36d).

Socrates' description of himself as a benefactor takes us back to the question of how can he help the city if, by his own admission, he is ignorant of the theories he wants to know. At *Gorgias* 521e–522b, he compares his plight to that of a doctor arguing against a pastry chef in front of a jury of children. The points of comparison are obvious save one: the doctor is in possession of a science (*technē*) which has the welfare of the children in mind.[30] Socrates may have the welfare of the city in mind, but he does not have nor claim to have the doctor's expertise. The problem may be viewed from a different light. The *Apology* leaves no doubt that Socrates thought of himself as virtuous—perhaps the best example of virtue the city has to offer.[31] That is why he can suggest with a straight face that no greater good ever came to the city than his service to god (30a), that he be put up in the Prytaneum for the rest of his life (36d–e), and that he does not fear death because no evil can befall a good person either in this life or the next (41c–d). How is he able to say all this if he still does not have knowledge of virtue? If the purpose of *elenchus* is therapeutic, if being brought to shame really does make one a better person, does Socrates not require some sort of moral theory to show this? If, on the other hand, he persists in maintaining his ignorance, why should the jury believe him when he describes himself as its benefactor? It is to these questions that we now turn.

Notes to Chapter Three

1. Isocrates' *Antidosis* mimics the *Apology* time and again, e.g., 27, 33, 92, 93, 100, 154, 179, 240, 321.
2. John Burnet, *Plato's Euthyphro, Apology of Socrates, and Crito* (Oxford: Clarendon Press, 1924), 66–67.
3. R. Hackforth, *The Composition of Plato's Apology* (Cambridge: Cambridge University Press, 1933), 55–57.
4. Cf. W. K. C. Guthrie, *A History of Greek Philosophy*, Vol. IV (Cambridge: Cambridge University Press, 1975), 74: "When Socrates begins by disclaiming any skill in oratory, and tells the court to expect nothing but the unadorned truth, because he is entirely unfamiliar with the ways of lawcourts and can only speak in his accustomed homely manner, we might think that this is the genuine Socratic irony and not the way

anyone else would talk—until we learn that to conciliate the dicasts by pleading inexperience and depreciating the deceptive fluency of the other side was simply to follow the accepted rules.''

5. Heinrich Gomperz, *Sophistik und Rhetorik* (Leipzig: Teubner, 1912), 9–11. Since Gomperz, it has been assumed that the *Apology of Palamedes* antedates the *Apology of Socrates*. I can find no reason to challenge this assumption.

6. Kathleen Freeman, *Companion to the Pre-Socratic Philosophers* (Oxford: Blackwell, 1951), 363.

7. Guido Calogero, ''Gorgias and the Socratic Principle: *Nemo Sua Sponte Peccat*,'' *Journal of Hellenic Studies* 77 (1957), 12–17. The problem with this aticle is that it puts Gorgias in the position of being Socrates' teacher rather than the person Socrates is trying to parody. This would make Socrates' criticism of Gorgias in the *Gorgias* virtually impossible to understand.

8. This view is taken by A. H. Chroust, *Socrates, Man and Myth* (London: Routledge & Kegan Paul, 1957), 216–18.

9. James A. Coulter, ''The Relation of the *Apology of Socrates* to Gorgias' *Defense of Palamedes* and Plato's Critique of Gorgianic Rhetoric,'' *Harvard Studies in Classical Philology* 68 (1964): 269–303. This is the best study of the line by line similarities between the two texts. For criticism of Coulter, see Guthrie, *op cit.*, 76–8. I agree with Guthrie that Coulter is wrong in calling Plato's *Apology* an ''adaptation'' of Gorgias' *Palamedes*. The problem with this view is, as Guthrie indicates, that it ignores the extent to which the Socrates of the *Apology* is Gorgias' critic. That is why the parody interpretation is to be preferred.

10. *Palamedes* 5. All references to the works of Gorgias are from Diels and Krantz, *Die Fragmente der Vorsokratiker*, 16th ed., II. 82. B. 11 & 1a. I have supplied an English translation in the Appendix to this book.

11. *Phaedrus* 273b–c. But Aristotle (*Rhetoric* 1402a7) attributes this claim to Corax.

12. Cf. Isocrates, *Panegyricus* 8.

13. *Palamedes* 4. Cf. *Antidosis* 26.

14. The source of this tradition is *Gorgias* 486a–b, 521e–522b. But it takes a real leap of faith to think that these passages refer to the historical Socrates.

15. See Thucydides' *History* 1. 1. 22.

16. Burnet, *Plato's Euthyphro*, 63–66. The view that the *Apology* is largely fanciful was more popular in the nineteenth century, e.g., with Schantz, than it is today. To some extent, it has been resurrected by Chroust, *ibid.* For a more recent discussion, see R. E. Allen, *Socrates and Legal Obligation* (Minneapolis: University of Minnesota Press, 1980), 3–35. The strongest reason for holding that Plato's account cannot be completely fanciful is that he is the only author of an apology of Socrates who was actually present at the trial (*Apology* 34a, 38b). But even this is not decisive, and the debate continues.

17. Allen, *Socrates and Legal Obligation*, 8.
18. *Gorgias* 454e. For more on this point, see Coulter, "Relation," 286 ff. and Allen, 10–13.
19. Xenophon, *Memorabilia* 1. 2. 31 cf. *Gorgias* 450b–c.
20. There are, however, two places where Socrates does use appeal to probability: 25c–26a and 27b–d, both in the examination of Meletus. I think it is clear that Socrates is not using the normal standards of rigor in this section of the dialogue. On this point, Burnet, *op. cit.*, 106–7 writes: "Socrates does not condescend to use serious arguments against Meletus; his purpose is simply to show that his accuser does not understand his own *antōmosia* [affidavit]. It is not to the point, then, to complain that the arguments are 'sophistical.' It was legitimate and necessary for Socrates to show that the ostensible charge was a mere pretext, and that could be most effectively done by making it clear that the nominal prosecutor did not even know what it meant. It was perfectly fair to lay traps for him in order to bring this out." For this point I am indebted to T. Nadler. See his reply to me in *Philosophy and Literature* 9 (1985), 198–201.
21. Cf. Allen, *Socrates and Legal Obligation* 6–7. But is not true, as Allen suggests several times, that Socrates did not deny the charges against him. This point will be discussed in greater detail in the next chapter.
22. E. R. Dodds, *Plato* Gorgias: *A Revised Text with Introduction and Commentary* (Oxford: Clarendon Press, 1959), 225. On the issue of freedom and degradation, see Terence Irwin, *Plato's* Gorgias: *Translated with Notes* (Oxford: Clarendon Press, 1979), 116–17, 136. Also see Socrates' references to freedom and slavery at *Theaetetus* 172e ff.
23. W. K. C. Guthrie, *A History of Greek Philosophy*, Vol. 3 (Cambridge: Cambridge University Press, 1969), 193 ff., thinks this treatise should be viewed seriously. The main difficulty in accepting Guthrie's opinion is that neither Plato nor Aristotle seem to have shared it. For additional criticism of Guthrie, see John M. Robinson, "On Gorgias," in Lee, Mourelatos, and Rorty, eds., *Exegesis and Argument* (New York: Humanities Press, 1973) 49–60.
24. For a good discussion of this passage, see Rudolph H. Weingartner, *op. cit.*, 95–102.
25. Jacqueline de Romilly, *Magic and Rhetoric in Ancient Greece* (Cambridge: Harvard University Press, 1975), 25.
26. Burnet, *Plato's Euthyphro*, 66–67.
27. Aristotle, *Rhetoric* 1419b4.
28. Dodds, *Plato Gorgias*, 8.
29. Allen, *Socrates and Legal Obligation*, 12.
30. For Socrates' understanding of the epistemological status of medicine, see *Gorgias* 464b ff. Notice that the distinction between a science (*technē*) and a knack (*empeiria*) is partly moral. The person with a science can give

an account of her subject and has the best interest of the patient in mind (464e–465a), cf. *Gorgias* 500a–b, *Republic* 342b ff.

31. Cf. Kraut, *Socrates and the State*, 268. But it will become clear in the next chapter that my explanation for this fact is different from his. Also see T. C. Brickhouse and N. D. Smith, "The Origin of Socrates' Mission," *Journal of the History of Ideas* (1983), 657–66.

Chapter Four
Socrates as Hero

DESPITE ITS APPEAL AS a rhetorical masterpiece and a parody of existing rhetoric, the *Apology* is difficult to interpret. The main reason for this is that Socrates does not say what we expect him to. If asked to write a speech on Socrates' behalf, we would have him state what the charge is—impiety—and formally deny it:

> The indictment charges me with impiety. All of you know that I have never robbed a temple, never murdered anyone, never broken an oath made on a god's name, never done anything which would normally be called impious. You know, too, that I have attended all of the state-sponsored festivals and never spoken ill of them. In what sense, then, are my actions impious?

That he does not do anything like this has puzzled people for centuries. Crito openly disapproves of the way he conducted his defense (*Crito* 45e), while Xenophon maintains he was getting ready to die (*Apology* 23). In the nineteenth century, Schanz argued that it was not really a defense at all.[1] Numerous scholars have taken issue with Socrates' reference to the Delphic Oracle.[2] More recently, Reginald Allen maintained that Socrates not only did not but could not answer the charges against him.[3] For if he does not know what piety is, how can he defend himself against the claim that his actions are *im*pious?

Of all these views, the last one raises the most serious question. If Socrates does not answer the charge of impiety, why does he go to such great lengths to describe himself as a benefactor to Athens and the loyal servant of god? On the other hand, if he does defend himself against the charge, does this not imply he has knowledge, thereby undermining his admissions of ignorance? Whatever the actual date of the *Apology*, the dramatic date is very late: it is Socrates' reflection on the meaning and purpose of his life. I will try to show that the

73

Apology does put forward a conception of piety according to which Socrates is the consummate religious hero. It is, then, a serious defense. But the conception of piety it puts forward does not imply that Socrates is in possession of a moral science; on the contrary, it is based on the observation that his attempts to found such a science have failed.

1. THE CONTEXT OF THE TRIAL

According to Socrates, there were, in effect, two sets of charges against him. The "old" charge, originating from Aristophanes' portrait of him in the *Clouds,* holds that Socrates is a wise man who investigates things in the air and below the earth and makes the weaker argument defeat the stronger (18b). Against the background of this prejudice, the "new" charge, that is, the legal indictment brought by Anytus, Meletus, and Lycon, states that Socrates is guilty of corrupting the youth, introducing gods of his own invention, and not recognizing (*nomidzein*) the official gods of the State (*Euthyphro* 3b, *Apology* 24b). Unfortunately, there is no English equivalent for *nomidzein*, and under the circumstances, it is difficult to say what his accusers meant by it. Is the problem that Socrates did not honor and respect the gods in an appropriate way, that he believed in gods but not the official ones of Athens, or that he was an atheist who did not believe in any gods at all?[4] Meletus opts for the latter (26c–e), but gives every impression of being confused.

What would it take to recognize the official gods in an appropriate way? The problem is that we do not know and it is likely that many of Socrates' contempories did not know either. Impiety, as M. I. Finley once argued, was a notoriously loose concept in Socrates' day.[5] It could mean anything from desecrating a temple to revealing the secrets of a mystery cult to saying things which cast the gods in a bad light. The reason is that Greek religion did not resemble a modern faith. It had little in the way of a formal doctrine or creed, no professional priesthood, no church hierarchy, no established schools of theology. We know from the *Euthyphro* (6a–b), that Socrates was skeptical of the old mythology, but so were a lot of others. The state continued to sponsor religious festivals and spend money on shrines. Yet such outward displays of piety could not hide the fact that the period was one of upheaval. As Nilsson tells us: "The old gods had been overthrown by criticism: they continued to exist only in public policy and in the minds of the simple and credulous, whom discus-

sions of the time passed by."[6] It is not surprising, therefore, that
Euthyphro expreses no alarm on hearing Socrates' skepticism and
never suggests that Socrates is guilty of a religious offense. On the
contrary, it is Euthyphro, who believes such stories, who is laughed
at in public (3b–c).

Upon hearing the charge against Socrates, Euthyphro infers that
the whole matter has to do with Socrates' *daimōn* or divine sign (3b).
This is the strange voice which comes to Socrates and warns him
against future courses of action. It is described at *Apology* 31c–d:[7]

> . . . you have often heard me say before on many occasions
> that a divine or supernatural experience comes to me, an ex-
> perience which Meletus mocked in his indictment. It began in
> childhood, some sort of voice which comes to me; and when
> it comes, it always dissuades me from doing what I am about
> to do, it never urges me on.

According to Euthyphro, this voice or sign is the "new god" which
Socrates is accused of putting in place of the official gods of the State.
Note that as orthodox a believer as Euthyphro does not interpret the
sign this way. At 3b–c, he expresses sympathy for Socrates and suggests that the two of them are in a similar position. The fact is,
however, that Socrates did not ask other people to worship the sign,
did not claim that it conferred on him some kind of elevated status,
and did not say that it revealed a body of special, religious
knowledge. It is likely that, as Euthyphro suspects, Meletus is a
scoundrel who has used the sign as a pretext for bringing Socrates into court. Then, as now, there were hordes of people claiming to
receive divine communication.[8] Euthyphro himself is an obvious example. But we know that formal charges of impiety were relatively
rare.[9]

What, then, is the real reason for Socrates' trial? The answer is, in
part, a political one, but we should keep in mind that politics and
religion were mixed. A generation earlier, an indictment of impiety
was brought against Anaxagoras to embarrass Pericles. But Anaxagoras was not an Athenian and accepted exile. In 399 Athens was
recovering from defeat at the hands of the Spartans, and ambitious
politicians were looking for scapegoats. There is no need to go into a
long exposition of why Socrates was the scapegoat *par excellence*.
Unlike Anaxagoras, he was an Athenian. He was poor, ugly, and by
his own admission (*Apology* 17d, 32a–b, *Gorgias* 473c), a stranger to
the in's and out's of local politics. His association with Critias and

Alcibiades did not help his popularity, nor did his distrust of democracy. But the fact that he was an easy target is only half the story. Whatever the political motivations for Socrates' indictment, a subject on which Plato is strangely silent, it is undeniable that the old religion had been under attack for some time. The Milesian philosophers had argued that the world was governed by material principles which, though described in a god-like way, were far removed from Zeus and Hera. Xenophanes had proposed a version of monotheism or pantheism which had the obvious implication that traditional religion was nothing but superstition. In Athens, young aristocrats were flaunting disrespect for the gods. Eventually the mystery rites were profaned and the scared statues of the city mutilated. Was there any connection between philosophical speculation and disrespect for authority? The Athenians must have thought so because they outlawed the study of astronomy and went forward with the prosecution of Anaxagoras. James Beckman writes:[10]

> The defenders of the *polis* could no longer be satisfied with mere external compliance with public ritual. They were shrewd enough to perceive the radical implications for the political establishment of the new critical attitude toward the gods. To undermine the unquestioning acceptance of the traditional mythically conceived gods was ultimately to undermine the unquestioning acceptance of the form of the polis—for the gods were a basic element in the official theology, i.e., self-understanding of the state. Theoretically, at least, it was through the gods that the contingent social-political order was grounded in the timeless holy.

Despite the fact that Socrates *left* the school of Anaxagoras, and from everything we know, was deeply religious, participating in all required forms of worship, he was associated with the breakdown of traditional values.[11] In the *Meno* (94e–95a), Anytus flies into a rage when Socrates raises questions about the way the Athenians educate their young.

In short, Socrates personified the spirit of rational inquiry at a time when people regarded such inquiry as a threat. We can write off his accusers as a gang of ruthless politicians, but the question raised by the accusation cannot be handled in as hasty a fashion. No court could take issue with Socrates' conviction that virtue is the greatest good a person can acquire. If he had discovered the moral theory he was searching for, if he could identify the foundation from which such convictions spring, he could defend his life by pointing to an un-mistakable accomplishment. Here is the moral theory which will bring the Athenians back to their senses, to serving the gods, obeying the laws, not going to excess in the pursuit of food or drink, and facing danger with resolve. But he failed; and that casts a different light on the legitimacy of his enterprise. Consider the argument of Peter Geach.[12] Suppose an impressionable youth is asked to define justice. He answers that swindling is unjust. Socrates shows in the usual way that one cannot define a virtue by citing examples. Before long, it is clear that the youth does not have an acceptable definition of justice. Without such a definition, he cannot be sure that swindling or anything else is an example. So when the opportunity presents itself, he decides that swindling is not unjust and pursues a life of crime. This in a nutshell is why people thought Socrates had corrupted the youth. In the *Clouds*, Strepsiades sends his son to Socrates not to learn about virtue but to devise a technique for cheating creditors.

While the goal of *elenchus* may have been to secure a foundation for moral judgments, in practise it could easily do the opposite. As Socrates indicates, young people enjoy watching their elders succumb to refutation, and anyone who can do this with the skill of a Socrates is bound to have imitators (23c). It is likely that the imitators would ignore the positive side of the *elenchus* and concentrate on making fools of others. This would be particularly easy in the area of religion, where as we have seen, there was already a measure of confusion. Indeed, *confusion* may be too generous. To the degree that Euthyphro represents the orthodoxy of his day, it was nothing but a commercial relationship between gods and men (14e)—a travesty of religion ripe for Socratic examination.

2. SOCRATES' MISSON

Against this background, Socrates maintained that far from being an affront to the gods, philosophy is a way of serving them. This claim must have struck the jury as patently absurd. Was the philosophic tradition not responsible for the unbelief of men like Democritus and Protagoras? As for Socrates, how does one serve the gods by refuting widely held beliefs about morality and religion? It would be easier to defend Socrates if he had been a proponent of what we now call *natural theology*, the view that like botany or astronomy, theology is a science culminating in demonstrably true propositions. The only difference between it and other disciplines in that theology is about god; it provides a *logos* of the divine. According to Werner Jaeger, natural theology began with the Milesian thinkers so that if Socrates had wanted, he could have carried on the tradition of Thales and Xenophanes.[13] But there is no direct evidence in the early dialogues that Socrates engaged in theological speculation, and he never claimed to have knowledge of "higher" matters hidden from other people.[14] What Socrates claimed to have is *human* knowledge (*anthrōpinē sophia*, 20d). So the question remains: How does one serve the gods by talking about virtue and showing people they do not know what they think they do?

The answer is found at *Apology* 23a–d, when Socrates explains the meaning of the oracle:

> On each occasion, those present think I am wise in the matters on which I refute others. But quite likely, gentlemen, the truth is that it is god who is wise, and by his oracle, he means: "Human wisdom is a thing of little or no value." It appears that he does not mean Socrates in particular but merely uses my name as an example as if to say: "That man is wisest, gentlemen, who, like Socrates, recognizes that in respect of wisdom, he is really worthless."

In this way, the religious lesson of Scoratic philosophy is simple. Real wisdom is the province of god. It follows that the people who profess wisdom lay claim to something no mortal can have. Like the old tragic heroes, they have become so enamored of their accomplishments that they have lost sight of their limitations. They present themselves as experts when they are only repeating thet standard cliches.

At the bottom of this lesson is bitter irony. There is only one person in the city who does *not* profess wisdom, one person who goes about proclaiming his ignorance. It is well to remember, however, that Socrates' avowal of ignorance is not the result of indecision on moral questions. We have seen that no one was more convinced of the truth of what he was saying, and as far as the *Apology* is concerned, no one was more convinced of the benefits of his own behavior. His avowal of ignorance is his recognition that conviction, no matter how strong, does not entail knowledge. For the latter, a person must be able to give a *logos* or account—something which Socrates did not think he could do. He now finds himself on trial for impiety. Yet surely it is the others, the ones who think they are wise, who have committed a religious offense. For in claiming to know, they are claiming to have crossed the boundary which separates human achievement from divine. What is called a crossing is, from Socrates' standpoint, a transgression. In a word, it is the citizens of Athens who are guilty of *hubris*.

The best example of such *hubris* is, interestingly enough, Euthyphro. As the dialogue opens Euthyphro has come to the portico of the king-archon to file a complaint. When Socrates learns that Euthyphro is accusing his father, and that the charge is murder, he is amazed and assumes there must be a simple explanation. Perhaps Euthyphro's father has killed a relative. But to his surprise, Socrates learns that Euthyphro is prosecuting his father for the murder of a slave who, it turns out, has shed human blood himself. Socrates replies with an epistemological question (4e):

> In the name of Zeus, Euthyphro, is your knowledge of divine law and things holy and unholy so accurate that, if the facts are as you say, you can prosecute your father without fearing that it is you who are doing something unholy?

Euthyphro answers, without hesitation, that his knowledge of such things *is* exact and is why he is uniquely qualified to expound on the subject of piety.

A page or so later, he goes further. It is acknowledged that Zeus is the highest of the Olympian deities. But according to the old stories, Zeus puts his father in chains. Why do people get angry when Euthyphro tries to do the same thing? The answer is obvious: behavior appropriate to the highest of the Olympian deities may not be appropriate to a mortal. In fact, it is blasphemous for a mortal to assume that it is. In his fanaticism, Euthyphro has gotten everything backward. This is not to deny the possibility that a parent may be guilty of a religious offense and the resulting guilt (*miasma*) communicated to other members of the family. Socrates' position is not that Euthyphro's behavior is inherently objectionable; it is, rather, that Euthyphro's behavior presupposes certainty on matters which are probably beyond human comprehension. That is why the *elenchus* is so damaging to Euthyphro: it shows that he is not even close to mastering the knowledge his behavior requires.

While Euthyphro's legal stand may be extreme, his epistemological one is not. The city is full of people who have too high an opinion of themselves. Hence the reason for the Socratic mission: to find someone whose claim to wisdom is genuine. But after a lifetime of searching, he informs the jury that he has found nothing but arrogance and vanity. Here, then, is the religious dimension of Socratic philosophy, the reason he tells the jury that far from convincing him of a crime, it should be giving him its highest honor (36d). *Hubris* is an all too prevalent phenomenon. However inviolate the boundary between humans and god, it is easy for humans to lose sight of it. This tendency is dangerous not only because is angers the gods, but because it leads to a second, more serious offense.

In laying claim to something he does not have, the person who professes wisdom is ignorant of the most important fact of his existence—fallibility. He cannot even say that he has achieved the simple, human wisdom of Socrates: the recognition that he does not know. In this way, he violates the words written on the temple of Apollo: he does not know himself. According to Nilsson, these words would have been interpreted by the average Greek as meaning: ''Know that you are human and nothing more.''[15] It follows that the root of impiety is really ignorance—not ignorance of the truth Euthyphro claimed to have but ignorance of the true measure of one's worth.

The cure for such ignorance is, of course, philosophy. Though it may spread doubt and confusion at times, in the hands of Socrates, it at least spreads honesty. If so, we may compare a Socratic dialogue to a Greek tragedy. The respondent comes in beaming with confidence and unaware of what is about to happen. He encounters Socrates and makes light of the challenge before him. A contest ensues, but it is a contest we know the respondent cannot win. Eventually his claims to expertise are smashed, and he leaves the discussion in epistemological shambles. As Vlastos claims about Euthyphro, he ''. . . is as good as told that his failure to make good his confident claim to know 'exactly' (5a, 15d) what piety is, means not just that he is intellectually hard up, but that he morally bankrupt.''[16] It is clear, then, why Socrates thought that philosophy has a devine sanction (23b):

> I go about even now on behalf of the god, searching and inquiring among citizens and foreigners, whomever I think is wise. And when it seems to me he is not, I do a service to god by proving it.

If ignorance is the root of impiety, then knowledge is the root of piety. Again, this is not the super human knowledge of the natural theologian or the self-appointed seer but the recognition that if one is going to be honest with herself, then, like Socrates, she will have to confess ignorance.

Note the phrase *if one is going to be honest with herself.* The piety here envisioned asks one to disregard her standing in the community, her ability to please those around her, and face up to her limitations. Thomas Schmid is correct in saying that to achieve this sort of "humility before truth" one must be willing to endure ridicule, refutation, humiliation, and everything else that is involved in admitting that one's cherished beliefs are mistaken.[17] The road to this achievement is, of course, the *elenctic* process and its champion Socrates. The tragedy of the *Apology* thus goes beyond the fact that Socrates is about to die. It is that the one person in Athens who is truly innocent of a religious offense is being judged by the guilty and found wanting.[18]

3. KNOWING THAT ONE DOES NOT KNOW

Can we therefore conclude that Socrates has found an answer to the question "What is piety?" In one respect, the answer is no. When Socrates interprets the oracle as saying that human wisdom is of little or no value, he rules out the possibility that he has discovered a set of principles capable of regulating religious practise and belief.[19] Such a discovery could hardly be described as worthless. There is, then, no alternative but to take Socrates' confessions of ignorance seriously. If, as many commentators suppose, his confessions are insincere, his interpretation of the oracle would not be ironic, it would amount to a bold faced lie. Worse, it would undermine any possibility of defending himself against the charge of impiety for it would put him in the position of thinking he knows what only god can know.

On the other hand, we must be careful not to make so much of Socrates' confessions of ignorance that we attribute to him a theory about the limits of human understanding. Unlike Hume or Kant, Socrates has no arguments designed to establish skeptical conclusions. Rather than arguments, what he has is an observation based on a life time of asking questions. If the oracle is right, and he never doubts that it is (21b), Socrates is the wisest person in Athens.[20] If he has not found what he is searching for, there is reason to believe the task will remain unfinished—at least as far as the present life is concerned. The phrase "there is reason to believe" is not as precise as we might like. From the fact that Socrates has not found answers to his questions, it does not follow that no one else will. But it is as precise as the text allows. This does not mean that elenctic inquiry cannot make progress and will be forever stalled on the same points, only that we must approach it with drastically reduced expectations about the prospects for success. The *Republic* (540b–c) holds open the possibility that the process can be completed in an ideal state but goes on to say that if a person were to complete it, she would cease to be human and become a demi-god worthy of memorials and sacrifices. In the *Apology*, Socrates leaves no doubt that he *is* human and has not come close to this kind of perfection.

Drastically reduced expectations often conflict with scholarly claims that the pieces of the puzzle have come together. There is a long tradition of scholars claiming to find an acceptable definition of piety between the lines of the *Euthyphro*. Adam, putting great emphasis on 13e, argued that piety is a service to the gods in which we assist them in producing noble products.[21] Socrates does, of course, describe himself as a servant of god at 23b (quoted above). But what products could such service possibly produce? The only plausible alternative is to identify them with virtuous acts, in which case piety is service to the gods in the production of virtuous acts which *we* perform. The gods, presumably, do not need our help in performing virtuous acts of their own. As Vlastos put it: '' . . . since the gods are great and powerful past all imagining, they surely don't need our services to improve *their* estate; and since they are also good and benevolent, they do desire what is best for us—and what can this be, but the improvement of our souls?''[22] All those who think that service is the essence of piety face this question: If the gods do not need our help to improve their estate, exactly why do we need their help in improving ours? Suppose a person assisted others in performing virtuous acts but neither called on nor referred to divine guidance. If the goal of piety is improvement of the soul, why would such a person not qualify as pious? Put otherwise, why must a person who assists in the performance of virtuous acts trust, serve, or even believe in the gods? Unless we answer this question, we face the paradox that piety may be compatible with atheism. The truth is, however, that the *Euthyphro* is far from answering it. It is agreed that the gods love what is pious, but whether this love must be returned, and if so, how, the dialogue does not say.

A somewhat different approach has been taken by Laszlo Versényi. For him, speculation about what the gods do or do not produce is irrelevant:[23]

> . . . if the gods are by definition good, without knowing their precise attributes we can be certain that good action and con-

duct will be holy, pious, and pleasing to the gods. If so, piety is not a special virtue, but virtue itself becomes the essence of piety, and the good man, simply by virtue of this excellence, is *eo ipso* pious.

We can accept that the good man is *eo epso* pious. The question is: *why* is he pious? According to Versényi, *eusebia* (holiness) does not necessarily specify a relationship to the gods; it means awe, fear, or respect towards whatever is worthy of these emotions, be it human or divine.[24] This implies knowledge of good and evil so that on this analysis, piety is simply wisdom. Again the gods have dropped out of the picture: on Versényi's account, there is no reason why an agnostic like Protagoras could not qualify as pious. But there is also a textual problem: the *Euthyphro* does not set forth the principles on which such wisdom rests, and the Socrates of the *Apology* never says he knows what they are. So we are back to the old dilemma: either (a) Socrates is not pious and his defense is really an evasion, or (b) piety cannot be wisdom if the latter means a science (*epistēmē*, *Euthyphro* 14c) of how to comport oneself in respect to the divine.

I submit that (b) is the only reasonable choice. The *Apology* is Socrates' reflection on the fact that the *Euthyphro* and all similar discussions of virtue have come up short. In the context of reduced expectations, the only knowledge accessible to us is the human knowledge that comes with recognizing one's limitations. If, to repeat, real wisdom is the province of god, there is at least something of value in the realization that this is so. It took Socrates a lifetime to come to it and is the crux of his defense against the charge of impiety. He is pious not because he has superior knowledge of "higher" matters but because he does not overreach himself in claiming to know what he does not. We can call this a second order conception of piety to the degree it assumes a science of piety is beyond human capability. Notice that on this interpretation, the gods do not drop out of the picture. For Socrates, acknowledging the limits of human understanding is nothing but a way of acknowledging the superiority of divine. *Apology* 23a–b treats them as correlative. There is, then, no possibility of ignoring the gods and, like Protagoras, proclaiming man the measure of all things.

It is also worth noting that for Socrates, acknowledging the limits of human understanding is more than an epistemological truism. His position is *not* that the elenctic process may never be finished and therefore the only legitimate response is moral quietude. It is rather:

the elenctic process may never be finished and therefore the only legitimate response is to obey our superiors, namely the gods. At 29d he sounds very much like Antigone in saying that his loyalty to god is greater than his loyalty to the Athenian court. This statement stands together with his claim that philosophy is obedience to a divine command (28e, 33c). There is, then, more to Socrates' defense than the feeble attempt to show Meletus that anyone who believes in divine activities or effects also believes in divine beings (27b ff.) There is a genuine reverence for the gods and a willingness to admit that they rather than we are the ultimate moral authorities.[25] Thus Socrates' position is opposed to two things: (1) the agnosticism of Protagoras, which refuses to recognize the superiority of divine guidance, and (2) the fanaticism of Euthyphro, which admits the superiority of divine guidance but maintains that *he* is an infallible source for revealing it. Each of these alternatives is a way of ignoring human limitations.

4. PIETY AND THE OTHER VIRTUES: TEMPERANCE

There is a reason for engaging in Socratic conversation even if it is not that we are guaranteed to find a body of knowledge capable of resolving all moral disputes. The only thing Socrates can promise in the *Apology* is that we will be relieved of the false conceit of thinking we know when we do not. There is an obvious respect in which a person suffering from this conceit is doubly at fault: not only is she mistaken about what she claims to know, and must therefore go around with false beliefs about the virtues, but in thinking that her beliefs are true, she will have no reason to look for better alternatives. The trouble with false conceit is that it tends to perpetuate itself. But there is more than this. In the Socratic dialogues, it is false conceit which is responsible for the arrogance, vanity, and cowardice which appear on practically every page. Because they have a great deal invested in their answers, very few respondents submit calmly or reasonably to refutation. It could be said, therefore, that if Socrates' refusal to overreach himself has practical consequences for the way he lives his life, his respondents' eagerness to do so has practical consequences as well.

It is clear that *elenchus* is the proper antidote for such conceit, which is the reason Socrates can describe himself as a benefactor to the city. In the *Sophist* (230b –c), *elenchus* is said to be a way of settling and purifying a troubled soul—not because it puts the soul in contact with an indubitable reality but because it relieves the soul of the unyielding posture it has taken in regard to its own opinions. Without *elenchus*, false conceit is rampant, and with false conceit comes the impiety of claiming what only the gods have a right to claim.

Friedländer saw in the *Apology* a reference to the familiar Socratic notion that all of the virtues are ways of looking at one condition.[26]

> "Piety" is the over-all concept, and the speech ends with the strong affirmation: I revere the gods more than any of my accusers do (35d). Thus, by "reverence of the gods" Socrates means something very different from what his accusers mean. It is piety together with, or indissolubly linked with, justice, courage, and wisdom. The unity of the virtues is visible throughout, even if it is not stated as an explicit theme.

This suggestion is right to the degree that the conception of piety with which Socrates defends himself is linked to other forms of moral behavior. But we must be careful not to think that it is the key which unlocks all the other dialogues. Again, the *Apology* is Socrates' reflection on the fact that previous discussions of virtue have come up short.

Consider temperance. The connection between temperance and piety is best seen by noticing that the most serious candidate for a definition of temperance in the *Charmides* is a reformulation of the Delphic injunction: Know thyself.[27] Critias, a man whom history showed to be profoundly *in*temperate, interprets the Delphic injunction as synonymous with: Be temperate (164d–e). There is good reason for this interpretation. If knowing oneself means knowing one's limits, and if it assumed that *qua* human beings, we are all limited in significant respects, the Delphic injunction amounts to: Know your limits and do not exceed them. We can think of limits in a variety of ways: political, sexual, economic, etc., but the underlying assumption of elenctic inquiry is that the most important limit is intellectual: the fundamental human shortcoming being the false conceit of ignorance. It is clear, then, that the person who overreaches himself in claiming to know what he does not is intemperate as well as impious, an observation whose truth is revealed in the eccentric behavior and bombastic claims of Euthyphro as well as the murderous cruelty and professed atheism of Critias.[28]

In any case, Critias' definition of temperance is reformulated by Socrates as follows (*Charmides* 167a):

> Then the temperate person is the only one who will know himself and be able to examine what he knows and does not

know, and be able to see what others know and think they know, when they do know, and what they do not know and think they know, when they do not. No one else will be able to do this. And this is temperance and being temperate and knowing oneself—to know what one knows and what he does not.

This is an obvious reference to Socrates and accords with the human knowledge mentioned at *Apology* 20d. Assign such a person a lifetime of elenctic examination in Athens and she will come away thinking, like Socrates, that human knowledge does not amount to much. Indeed, the passage repeats, almost verbatim, Socrates' description of himself at *Apology* 21d.

It happens that Critias' definition is rejected in the *Charmides* and therefore cannot be taken as Socrates' final word on the subject of temperance. The details of this refutation are complex and need not concern us here. In outline the argument goes like this: Critias has defined temperance as a knowledge of self, which Socrates takes to mean knowledge which has itself as its object; in short a knowledge of knowledge. Socrates proceeds to ask how such knowledge would benefit us. Obviously it would pay us to know when people who claim expertise are telling the truth. But there is a problem with this. To determine whether a doctor knows what she is talking about, one would have to have the knowledge of a particular subject, namely health. Similarly with a farmer, architect, or other craftsman. But Critias' knowledge is not knowledge of a particular subject but knowledge which takes itself as its object. So this sort of knowledge would not enable one to decide whether people in the arts and crafts are telling the truth when they profess expertise. All one could do is decide whether other people who claimed to have knowledge of knowledge are tellling the truth. If we imagined a city in which this sort of knowledge held sway, then we would have a city in which no one claimed to know what she does not. But Socrates objects that this is not enough. What the citizens need to make them happy is not knowledge of knowledge but knowledge of good and evil. It follows that if temperance is advantageous, it cannot be identical with knowledge of knowledge which has been shown to be of questionable value.

We can object, with Schmid, that the argument gets off on the wrong foot.[29] *Elenchus* was never supposed to be a test of a person's technical competence but of her moral beliefs (*Apology* 22c–e). And we can also object that knowledge of knowledge is not a series of reflections on other subjects, but, in the most fundamental way, knowledge of the soul. But the dialogue provides very little insight into the nature of the soul whose improvement temperance is supposed to seek. For present purposes, all that matters is that both temperance and piety imply the honesty of being able to recognize one's limits. Both are opposed to the inflated self image Socrates tried to correct. Both require a sense of shame, the characteristic emotion Socrates produced. If Socrates does not have a science capable of regulating religious practice and belief, neither does he have a science of good and evil. The point is that in both cases, he has made a virtue of admiting he does *not* have it. This admission is what leads him to treat the gods as his superiors and listen to his respondents without becoming arrogant or resentful.

5. COURAGE

The connection between piety and courage, though not as obvious as the former one, is still present. Socrates' claim is that he has shown piety in putting aside the normal human concerns and becoming a servant of god. But the accusers are demanding that he abandon that service and give up the philosophical mission on which he is embarked. The threat that they hold out is death: if Socrates is found guilty of impiety, the accusers will ask that he be executed. His response is to point out that he has been in dangerous situations before and that to fear death is an example—perhaps the prime example—of overestimating one's knowledge. As we are told at 28d–29a:

> I would have done a terrible thing, men of Athens, if, when the generals you chose stationed me at Potidaea and Amphipolis and Delium, I remained there as others did and ran the risk of death. But then, when the god stationed me, as I thought and supposed, ordering me to devote my life to philosophy by examining myself and others, I then deserted my post through fear of death or anything else. It would be a terrible thing, and truly you would be right to bring me into court for not acknowledging the existence of the gods, for not believing the oracle, for being afraid of death, and for thinking myself wise when I am not. For the fear of death is nothing else than to think oneself wise when he is not; that is, it is thinking that one knows what he does not.

Note the connection: if Socrates fears death, he will be turning his back on god and therefore be guilty of impiety. Piety demands that one acknowledge god's superiority even in the face of danger. Therefore to abandon his mission is both cowardly and unholy.

In the *Laches*, (196c–d), Nicias defines courage as the knowledge of what is to be dreaded and what is to be dared. Upon examination, this definition is taken to mean the knowledge of future good and evil, which, in turn, is taken to mean the knowledge of good and evil simpliciter. Here, too, the definition is rejected. If courage is knowledge of good and evil simpliciter, it would be identical with all of virtue. Yet earlier (190c–d) Socrates and his respondents agreed it was only a part. It has been argued that this objection is really no objection at all if we take the unity of the virtues seriously. To this argument we may reply that the objection has force if we recognize that the early dialogues do not contain an adequate account of how individual virtues like courage are related to the whole. Is virtue a genus which contains its parts as mammal contains human, feline, and canine? If so, then virtue would not imply courage. From an understanding of mammal, one cannot deduce the existence of a two-footed rational mammal: a genus does not imply its differentia. Is virtue a concept whose meaning does imply one of its parts as even number implies two?[30] Or is it a generic term coextensive with each of its parts? Any of these relationships could explicate the statement that courage is a *part* of virtue. Socrates' objection forces us to raise this issue and suggests that until it is decided, we cannot claim to know what courage is or attribute such knowledge to Socrates.

Still, from the standpoint of the *Apology*, fear of dying is not a failure of nerve but a failure to admit ignorance, another form of *hubris*. For all we know, death may be a blessing. To disobey god rather than face death is to act *as if* one knew the latter is worse than the former: that it is better to be disloyal than to be dead. This attitude is for Socrates a delusion brought about by failure to examine conventional beliefs. The passage just quoted continues:

> . . . if I were to say that I was wise than others in anything it would be in this: that not having sufficient knowledge about the next world, I do not think I have it. But I do know that it is evil and shameful to do injustice and to disobey my superior, whether man or god.

As far as the *Apology* is concerned, Socrates has no proof that disobedience to god is more to be feared than death. He believes it with conviction, but he cannot demonstrate its truth. On the other hand, the coward certainly cannot demonstrate the converse: that death is more to be feared than disobedience. The difference is that the coward may never have examined his conviction; all he is interested in is saving his skin. The possibility that this belief may be wrong or the fact that it *is* a belief are realizations he has shut out.

It follows that we cannot define courage as knowledge of good and evil and stop there. Even if we could decide the logical problem of how courage is related to the whole of virtue, we would have to add two pieces of information in order to be faithful to the *Apology*: (1) that by the time of Socrates' death, no person had mastered this knowledge, and (2) therefore it is incumbent on us to obey our superiors. Once we acknowledge, as Socrates does repeatedly, that god is one of our superiors, courage and piety are linked. The *Apology* does not envision a situation in which we confront danger with complete understanding of good and evil or one in which we confront it without guidance from a superior. Socrates' point is that if we take the time to compare the conviction that our superior is right with our ability to predict what death has in store, no reasonable person will sacrifice everything to avoid death. Thus his defiant assertion that he will not give up his mission even if he had to die a hundred times (30b–c). This is nothing but Scorates' way of saying that since human knowledge is of little or no value, he has no choice but to obey god.

6. JUSTICE

The connection between the other virtues and justice is affirmed at 35c–d, when Socrates tells the jury that he will not appeal to their emotions in an attempt to gain acquittal. The jury does not sit to grant favors but to decide where justice lies. It would be both cowardly and impious for Socrates to ask the jury to decide the case on anything but the facts: "Therefore it is clear that if by persuasion and supplication I prevailed upon you to break your oath, I would teach you not to believe in the existence of the gods and in conducting my defense, would be accusing myself of not recognizing them."

This speech is important because in the next dialogue, Crito, a law-abiding citizen, tries to persuade Socrates to commit an act of injustice in order to save his skin.[31] Crito's argument is a hodgepodge of emotion, entreaty, and accusation, but the crucial point is this: Socrates will be playing the fool if he goes to his death and does not avail himself of the opportunity to escape from prison. In short, Crito is asking Socrates to disobey a superior, in this case the laws of Athens, and run away. The confused way in which Crito presents the argument indicates that he is deeply troubled, a fact confirmed by the introductory conversation (43a–b) where we learn that he has had trouble sleeping.

What follows is a paradigm example of *elenchus*. Without dictating to Crito, or asking him to agree to anything he does not believe, Socrates brings him back to his senses. Putting aside the question of death, he convinces Crito that it would be wrong to break the law. From the point of view of the *Apology*, Crito's argument is the result of unreasonable haste. He is not an evil man, but the events of the trial have so disturbed him that he has temporarily lost his senses. What the dialogue shows is the Crito is recommending a course of action opposed to his own considered judgments. We may conclude that his advice is not motivated by a perverse delight in unjust behavior but, in a literal sense, a moment of delusion. His feeling that Socrates should break the law presupposes that disobedience is not as bad as death, loss of face, or inability to support one's family. Contrary to what he tells Socrates (45e), it is Crito who has adopted the position of the coward, Crito who things he knows more about death than he really does.

The *elenchus* of the *Crito* shows how convincing people of their ignorance is a service to god—and, as the context reveals, to the state as well. The process of question and answer has a soothing effect. At the very end of the dialogue, when Socrates gives Crito the chance to speak against the conclusion at which they have arrived, Crito admits, with complete honesty, that he has nothing to say. It is not that he has mastered the science of good and evil—a lifetime of listening to Socrates has produced only modest results—but at least he is not muttering a host of things he does not understand and making preparations to break the law.

7. SOCRATIC PIETY

Did Socrates deny the charges against him? Not in the way the jury would have expected. The jury would have wanted to hear about sacrifices, oaths, shrines, and contributions. Socrates did not deny the charges in this sense. Nor did he deny them by claiming privileged access to god or knowledge beyond the reach of ordinary people. He did deny he was guilty of impiety in the sense in which impiety involves false conceit. And in so doing, he also denied that he was intemperate, cowardly, or unjust.

His discussions of these virtues in the *Euthyphro, Charmides, Laches,* and *Republic* I all end without a satisfactory definition. The problem is not one of interpretation: that if, to recall Grote's description, we could probe a little deeper, we could solve the problems Socrates raises. The *Euthyphro* does not hint at a solution to the problem of divine-human interaction nor does it contain a body of claims about the activities of divine beings. Like the *Charmides, Laches* and *Republic* I, it is and is meant to be a discussion which raises a question it cannot answer. As for Socrates, we have a man who, by confessing his ignorance, exhibits exemplary behavior. If he can get others to confess their ignorance, then based on the example he sets, he would be a benefactor to the city. To be sure, the knowledge he claims for himself is only human knowledge so that granting the connecton between virtue and knowledge, the virtue he exhibits would be human virtue. But then human virtue is enough to qualify as heroic just as human knowledge is enough to make one the wisest person in Athens.

To return to a theme discussed in the first chapter, the great optimism of Socrates' position is that we can pursue inquiry to the fullest without arousing the anger of the gods. The lesson of Socrates' life is that if we do, we will come to a realization of human limitation. Comparing Socrates to Oedipus, Bernard Knox argues that the latter came to a realization of human limits as well.[32] But Oedipus suffered greatly to get there. Whatever else Socrates does in the dialogues, he does not suffer. If Crito is walking the streets of Athens in the middle of the night, Socrates is sleeping like a baby. By the time he drinks the hemlock, he is the very picture of a successful life. As he tells his followers earlier in he *Phaedo* (69c–d):

> It seems as if those who established our mystery rites are not to be despised, but, in fact, have long been saying in riddles that whoever arrives in the next world impure and uninitiated will lie in the mud while he who arrives purified and initiated will dwell with the gods. For it is indeed true, as those involved with the initiations say, "The thrysus bearers are many, but the devotees few." Now the latter are, in my opinion, none other than those who have been true practitioners of philosophy. And I have striven by every means possible, and to the best of my ability, to be counted among them.

This passage is troubling not because it contradicts anything Socrates says in the *Apology* but because *we* are not used to hearing philosophers talk this way. Few contemporary philosophers would permit a comparison between themselves and a religious advocate or devotee. That Socrates advances just such a comparison is a sign that our conception of philosophy is not his. We do not necessarily think of ourselves as obeying a superior.

It does not follow that Socrates' conception of philosophy is right. It may be that contemporary practitioners of the art are well advised to insist on their secular prerogatives. The danger is in thinking that if we are the intellectual descendents of Socrates, then our conception must be present in his words, if not explicitly, then by implication. This attitude leads to a neglect of the religious dimensions of his thought, which, in turn, leads to the idea that he never really denied the charges against him. We will overlook much of Socrates' justification for doing philosophy unless we recognize that this idea is false.

Notes to Chapter Four

1. Schanz' position is quoted by Burnet, *op. cit.*, 64–5.
2. See, for example, Hackforth, *op. cit.*, 101–4. A more complete list and a sympathetic interpretation of Socrates mention of the oracle can be found in Brickhouse and Smith, *ibid.*
3. Reginald Allen, *Socrates on Legal Obligation, op. cit.*, 13–5.
4. According to Burnet, *op cit.*, 15, and Allen, *Plato's Euthyphro, op cit.*, 62, *nomidzein* refers not to belief in gods but to proper worsip of them. But this view has been refuted by J. Tate in "Greek for 'Atheism'," *Classical Review* 50 (1936), 3–5 and "More Greek for 'Atheism'," *Classical Review* 51 (1937), 3–6. For further discussion, see Guthrie *History of Greek Philosophy*, Vol. III, *op. cit.*, 237, n. 2 as well as James Beckman, *The Religious Dimension of Socrates' Thought* (Waterloo, Ontario: Canadian Corporation for Studies in Religion, 1979), 55–6.
5. M. I. Finley, *Aspects of Antiquity* (New York: Viking, 1960), 64.
6. Martin P. Nilsson, *Greek Piety*, translated by H. J. Rose (New York: Norton, 1969), 78.
7. For other references, see *Apology* 40a–c, *Phaedrus* 242b, *Republic* 496c, *Theaetetus* 151a. The literature on this experience is vast and not always very good. I do not think that Socrates' divine sign is a concession to the irrational or a type of revelation in the biblical sense. The best overall discussion, and perhaps, the soberest, is that of Beckman, *op. cit.*, 76–7.

8. On the prevalence of divine communication, see Xenophon, *Memorabilia* 1. 1. 3. But I am in agreement with Burnet *op. cit.*, 15–6, that despite Euthyphro's hunch, the divine sign could hardly have been the reason Socrates was brought to trial.

9. On this point, see Coleman Phillipson, *The Trial of Socrates* (London: Stevens, 1926), chapter 10.

10. Beckman, *op. cit.*, 67.

11. Xenophon, *Memorabilia* 1. 1. 2, 1.1. 19, 1. 3. 1.

12. Geach, *ibid.*

13. Jaeger, *The Theology of the Early Greek Philosophers* (Oxford: Clarendon Press, 1947).

14. It may be argued that this picture is contradicted by Xenophon (*Memorabilia* 1.4), who portrays Socrates as advancing a version of the argument from design. According to the *Phaedo* (97b ff.), Socrates rejected materialist theories of the universe because they ignored final causality. But Xenophon's picture of him is a long way from the *Phaedo*'s. In the *Phaedo*, Socrates believes in final causality as a principle of explanation; in the *Memorabilia*, he is well into the realm of speculative theology. There are two explanations for this: (1) Xenophon sought to defend Socrates against the charge of impiety and attributed to him beliefs which he did not hold. (2) Xenophon was extrapolating from the passage in the *Phaedo*. In either case, Xenophon's portrait is not confirmed by the early dialogues. A. R. Lacey goes so far as to doubt that the *Phaedo*'s concern with teleological explanation is really Socratic either. See "Our Knowledge of Scorates," in Vlastos (ed.), *op. cit.*, 43–4. For an opposing view, see Gulley, "The Philosophy of Scorates," *op. cit.*, 179–192. Gulley's main point is that the arguments in the *Memorabilia* have little or no parallel in the Pre-Socratics, the *Timaeus* and *Laws*, or the writings of Aristotle. But surely this weakens the claim that they are Socratic.

My own position is much closer to that of Laszlo Versényi, *Socratic Humanism* (New Haven: Yale Univ. Press, 1963), 106: "Unlike Xenophanes and Heracleitus, he simply refuses to engage in an inquiry into the essential nature of the gods. In the best Protagorean manner, he follows the accepted religious practices, leaving etiological explanations, rationalizations of myths and all speculation concerning the gods to others with more leisure and cleverness. As for him, he prefers to 'do his own,' reflect on his own nature and concentrate his inquiry on man rather than on divine matter. 'I am not yet able . . . to know myself and so it seems ridiculous to me, who does not even know this to inquire into irrelevant matters. And so I dismiss all these and, following the customary belief about them, reflect not on those but on myself . . .' (*Phaedrus* 229e – 230 A). Theological speculation as to the exact nature of the gods is not only difficult and obscure but also useless and irrelevant to Socrates because, in the manner of contemporary enlightenment, he refuses to believe that the gods can do or be anything but good . . . " I agree that

Socrates left theological speculation to Protagoras. Socrates did not profess agnosticism about the existence of the gods: Protagoras, to the best of my knowledge, never described himself as a religious hero in the manner of *Apology* 23b and *Phaedo* 69c-d. For Protagoras' agnosticism, see *Theaetetus* 162d as well as Diels and Krantz A 12. 4. For further discussion, see Jaeger, *op cit.*, 189. For more on atheism and agnosticism in the fifth century, see Guthrie, *op. cit.*, 226–49.

15. Nilsson, *op. cit.*, 47.
16. Vlastos, "The Paradox of Socrates," *op. cit.*, 6.
17. W. Thomas Schmid, "Socratic Moderation and Self-Knowledge," *Journal of the History of Philosophy*, 21 (1983), 339–348.
18. Cf. W. G. Rabinowitz, "Platonic Piety: An Essay Toward the Solution of an Enigma," *Phronesis* 3 (1958), 120: "The monstrousness of the Athenians' treatment of Scorates, for Plato, lay in this: that they had condemned and put to death for impiety a man who . . . had practiced the true piety of dialectic all his life." But I cannot agree that the *Euthyphro* contains a cryptic message according to which *nous* is to be substituted for "the gods." To make this argument, Rabinowitz has to rely on passages from Anaxagoras and the later dialogues of Plato. On my view, Socrates is at pains to call attention to the limitations of human reason and never suggests that anything can be substituted for "the gods."
19. I say this in opposition to the interpretation advanced by Taylor, *Plato: The Man and His Work* (1926; rpt. London: Methuen, 1966),) 148. According to Xenophon (*Mem.* 4.6 4), Socrates defined piety as knowledge of the law as it pertains to the gods. But this definition is vacuous until the notion of law is fleshed out. On Xenophon's authority, see n. 14 above.
20. Socrates is confused about what the oracle *means* but not about its truth. So it is not true, as Burnet, *op. cit.*, 92, implies, that Socrates set out to prove that oracle a liar. Oracular pronouncements were notorious for obscurity. For further discussion, see H. W. Parke, "Chaerephon's Inquiry about Socrates," *Classical Philology* 56 (1956), 249–50.
21. J. Adam, *Plato's Euthyphro* (Cambridge: Cambridge University Press, 1908), xii-xvii. Adam is followed by Brickhouse and Smith, ibid. The most decisive refutation of this view is that of Allen, *Plato's Euthyphro, op. cit.*, 6–9.
22. Vlastos, "The Paradox of Socrates," *op. cit.*, 14.
23. Versényi, *op. cit.*, 106–7.
24. Versényi, *op. cit.*, 107.
25. Cf. *Phaedo* 62b: "The gods are our keepers . . . "
26. Paul Friedländer, *Plato: The Dialogues . . . First Period*, trans. by H. Meyeerhoff (New Yorkz; Bollingen, 1964), 165. But having seen such a valuable point, why does Friedlander fail to mention temperance?
27. On this issue, I am indebted to Schimd, *ibid*. Also see T. G. Tuckey, *Plato's Charmides* (Cambridge: Cambridge Univ. Press, 1951), 9–10.

28. On the subject of Critias' atheism, see Guthrie, *op. cit.*, 243–4.
29. Schimd, *ibid.*
30. This example is taken from Allen, *Plato's Euthyphro, op. cit.*, 84–5. The part/whole relation may be understood, see Kraut, *op. cit.*, 261–2.
the latter without referring to the former. The definition of even number is a number evenly divisible by two. For further discussion of how the part/whole relation may be understood, see Kraut, op. cit., 261–2.
31. This point is also made by Drew Hyland, "Why Plato Wrote Dialogues," op. cit., 445. Hyland is here following the general line of argument advanced by Leo Strauss in *The City and Man* (Chicago: University of Chicago Press, 1964.
32. Knox, *op. cit.*, 194.

Chapter Five
Socrates as Teacher

T HIS CHAPTER MUST BEGIN with a qualification: the last word of the title ought to be in scare quotes since it is an important part of Socrates' epistemology that teaching in the usual sense of the term is impossible. If we broaden our understanding of *teach* to include *elenchus*, then in keeping with the spirit of Socratic philosophy, and the way Plato presents it, it is not enough to talk about teaching in the abstract. There must be a passage in which it is exhibited and not just described. Such a passage is the one in which Socrates examines Meno's slave on the subject of how to double the area of a square. In this chapter, I propose to follow a number of scholars in treating the examination of the slave as a paradigm of elenctic inquiry. A discussion of the broader context in which this examination occurs can be found in the next chapter.

The immediate context is this. After repeated failure in attempting to define virtue, Meno responds with the paradox that now bears his name (80d):

> How will you inquire into something, Socrates, if you don't have any idea what it is? What sort of things among those things you don't know will you establish as the object of your inquiry? And even if you are lucky enough to bump into it, how will you know that this is the thing you didn't know?

Socrates responds by connecting Meno's objection with a sophistical puzzle designed to show that inquiry is impossible:[1]

> I understand what you are trying to say, Meno. Do you see that this is a captious argument you introduce—that therefore a person cannot inquire into what he knows or into what he doesn't know? For he would not inquire into what he knows, since he knows it and there is no need of such inquiry. Nor

would he inquire into what he doesn't know, for he does not even know what he is inquiring about.

So interpreted, the paradox can be expressed as a dilemma: Either a person knows something or she does not. If she knows it, there is no need to inquire. If she does not know it, she will not know what to inquire about. Therefore inquiry is either superfluous or impossible.

Socrates' reply is to repeat a religious teaching he has heard from priests and preistesses. The soul is immortal and has been born many times. It has seen everything in this world and the next and has learned all things. Therefore what people call *learning* is in fact *recollection*. Since all nature is akin (*syggenēs*), there is nothing to prevent the soul, having recalled one piece of knowledge, to recall all the rest.

Not surprisingly, Meno is puzzled and asks Socrates to teach him that this is true. Socrates maintains that the thrust of what he has just said is that teaching is impossible; therefore if he were to teach Meno that it is true, he would be contradicting himself. Instead of proving that the theory of recollection is true, or asking Meno to accept it on faith, Socrates goes on to claim that it is a reasonable way of accounting for a curious fact: that a randomly selected slave can be led to see an important mathematical result if he is asked the right questions.

Although the ensuring discussion is one of the most memorable in the Platonic corpus, it is not miraculous. The boy makes several mistakes and at one point is reduced to silence. Socrates makes use of diagrams to enable him to see what is happening. More important, it is unlikely that the boy would ever solve the puzzle unless Socrates suggested to him that he consider the diagonal of the original square. The important point, however, is that the boy turns out to be the perfect respondent. He speaks freely, without putting on airs, and remains courteous to Socrates throughout the examination. He is, in other words, a better resopndent than his master and far better than most of the rich and famous men Socrates questions elsewhere. We will see later that this may present a difficulty for Socrates, but for now we must look at the text.

1. GETTING OFF ON THE WRONG FOOT

The problem Socrates gives him is how to double the area of a square. He begins by asking the boy to recollect a few general features about squares such as size, shape, etc. But the problem is introduced in such a way that the boy is almost certain to end up in a blind alley.

Socrates draws a square two feet on a side and establishes that its area is four feet. The boy then admits it would be possible to have a square twice as big and that its area would be eight feet. In asking about the side of the eight foot square (82d–e), Socrates creates two false impressions: (1) he suggests that there is an analogy between the four foot and the eight foot square so that if the first is generated from a two foot line, the second, being twice as big, ought to be generated from a four foot line, (2) by using round numbers and asking the boy to perform simple arithmetical operations, he suggests that the problem has an arithmetical solution. But of course the problem does *not* have an arithmetical solution because the line needed to generate an eight foot square is incommensurate with the side of a four foot square. Not surprisingly, the boy answers that to double the size of a square, one must double the side.

The reader is inclined to ask why Socrates has practically guaranteed that the boy will get off on the wrong foot. The answer is that he would not do this if his only concern was to see that the boy came to believe a true proposition. All he would do is state that an arithmetical solution is impossible and move directly to the notion of a diagonal. But Socratic inquiry does not work this way. If the boy is to be convinced that an arithmetical solution is impossible, he will have to see it on his own.

This point is made at 82e when, after the boy's first answer, Socrates interrupts the discussion to say that he is not teaching him anything, only asking questions. Bluck is right in claiming that we would have expected such a remark not after an incorrect response but a correct one.[2] Yet, he continues, the purpose of Socratic inquiry is not merely to replace false propositions with true; it is to help the respondent see *why* they are false and put himself in a better position to look for the truth. So while the boy's first answer is rejected, it is not irrelevant to the rest of the inquiry. Doubling the side of a square gives a figure that is too large. Therefore if the original square has a side of two, the line he is looking for must be greater than two but less than four. His next answer is three.

But this answer, too, does not work. Not only can the square not be doubled by increasing its side in the ratio of 1:2, it cannot be doubled by increasing it in the ration of 2:3. The inquiry, continued on these lines, would lead to the question of whether any ration of one integer to another will do—that is, to the question of incommensurability.[3]

By 84a, the slave has examined three squares: two, three, and four feet on a side. We have already seen that there is no way he can deduce a solution from the information he has; nor can he get to one by analyzing the meaning of the terms Socrates has provided.[4] If the desired result must be smaller than four but larger than two, and if three is incorrect, it will not do to look for integers. The boy must stop thinking about integers and look for a line.[5] Socrates suggests this at 84a, when he says that if the boy cannot calculate the answer, he can point to the line which will generate the required result. This suggestion does not give the answer away, it only provides a hint of where to look for it. But the boy is too confused to see what Socrates is getting at.

Socrates' remarks at 84b that by making a person feel perplexed, numbing him as it were, he is doing him a service because he has removed the false conceit of thinking one knows when one does not. Like Meno, the slave speaks freely when he does not know the answer and does not show any sign of hesitation until the *elenchus* is well under way. It is not until 84a that the slave recognizes the true state of his ignorance. In keeping with Bluck's remark that Socrates draws a lesson *before* the boy reaches a correct response, it is noteworthy that Socrates' point about the benefits of inquiry occurs at the moment of maximum confusion. The implication is that even if the examination had ended at 84b with the slave still confused, Socrates would be able to claim he had done the boy a service. Thus the purpose of inquiry is twofold: both to seek a solution and to relieve the false conceit of ignorance. In the *Sophist* (230c–d), Plato underscores the twofold nature of inquiry by claiming that only when the soul is purged of false conceit can it derive any benefit from knowledge. So once again, the moral significance of inquiry cannot be ignored.

2. ELENCTIC EDUCATION

Once Socrates introduces the notion of a diagonal, it takes the boy only a few minutes to see that the diagonal of the four foot square is the side of the eight foot square. One must be careful, though, not to credit the boy with too much. There is a definite order to Socrates' questions (82e), various types of encouragement, and an extremely helpful hint. In fact, most of the boy's responses are of the simple yes or no variety. He resembles Meno to the extent that he begins the inquiry thinking he knows the answer, but not to the extent that he begins with a pompous speech. It is Socrates who does most of the talking. Why, then, does Socrates emphasize repeatedly that he is not teaching the boy anything? And why does Kierkegaard insist that if the boy makes a discovery, the boy, not Socrates, gets the credit? At a rudimentary level, Socrates is trying to make a distinction between his own methods and those of the sophists. We saw in discussing the *Palamedes*, that sophistical training relied on memory and imitations. In a Socratic exmaination, there are no speeches to memorize, no models to imitate, and no self-contained units of wisdom to appropriate.

But beyond the obvious point of difference, Socratic *elenchus* has the peculiar quality of allowing the respondent to certify when something is true—even when he is laboring under serious misconceptions. Although Socrates formulates the opinions, it is the boy who decides whether to affirm them. There are two reasons for this. Since one of the purposes of Socratic inquiry is to have the respondent admit ignorance, Socrates gives him maximum freedom to go in whatever direction he wants. That way he has only himself to blame if the direction proves unfruitful: everything follows from what *he* has admitted. Although most respondents follow Euthyphro (11c–d) in putting the blame on Socrates, it is they who are at fault. The inquiry is constructed so that the opinions expressed are, in a real sense, their own. It is in this light that we can understand Socrates' claim that the slave's opinions are "in" his soul (86a–b). We have seen that the metaphor of inherence or containment raises a number of problems. Minimally it means that the boy, not Socrates or Meno, takes responsibility for what is said. The opinions are his becuase he accepted them without any form of compulsion. According to Vlastos, the boy has been taught not to rely on Socrates's suggestions because Socrates' suggestions do not always work.[6] Hence the importance of leading the boy down two blind alleys. It follows that if the inquiry should fail, the boy must admit to a personal shortcoming: it is the opinions he has voiced which have run aground. On the other hand, if it succeeds, the boy will be completely convinced of the result. It will be *his* opinion rather than something handed to him by the teacher.

We may conclude that if *elenchus* puts moral demands on the respondent, it puts equally stringent demands on the questioner. She cannot dogmatize. She cannot put herself in the position of a judge.[7] She cannot ask the respondent to take something on faith. She cannot decide for herself what is self evident. She cannot do anything until she has won the respondent's approval by helping him to become satisfied with his own admissions.

The second reason the respondent vouches for truth is that the inquiry begins by assuming that in some sense, the respondent already knows the answer. The respondent may be mistaken, but he is never completely ignorant; he has the knowledge needed to make the right discriminations if only he is questioned in a proper way. So no matter how confused the respondent's opinion might seem, it is not worthless. It is noteworthy how patient Socrates is with the slave even when he knows the boy is making a mistake. The examination is never rushed and the boy is never insulted. A false opinion is not an insurmountable obstacle. From Socrates' standpoint, it is not nearly as bad an opinion which is insincere.

By allowing the respondent to certify the truth of what is said, elenctic education assumes that the respondent's opinions have some value. They are the views of a person who has a partial grasp of the truth but is having trouble seeing it clearly. Socrates' explanation for the slave's coming to the right solution is not that he (Socrates) has performed a magnificent feat but that the slave must always have had the opinions he expressed because no one taught him geometry (85d–e). In short, Socrates does exactly what Kierkegaard's remark would lead us to expect: he gives as much credit as possible to the slave.

The fact that the opinions expressed by the slave are his, and have *always* been his, is offered as an explanation for two things: the slave's learning how to double the size of a square and Socrates' claim that inquiry is worthwhile. In regard to the latter, the examination is supposed to be a case of successful inquiry and therefore evidence that inquiry is possible. Some people have objected that the present passage proves nothing because, unlike his position in the dialogues, Socrates knows the answer to his question. The objection overlooks two points. First, that in the examination of Crito, Polus, and Callicles, Socrates may not *know* the answer but strongly believes he has found it. Thus the reference to adamant and steel at *Gorgias* 509a. But there is still an analogy to cases where such conviction is lacking. The significance of the present passage is not so much that Socrates already knows the answer but that Meno does. Meno can therefore direct his attention away from the mathematical problem to the larger issue of recollection. What Meno has to be convinced of is that the soul has opinions not immediately at its disposal and that there is an orderly way of bringing them to light. So even if there is a difference between Socrates' examination of the slave and his examination of Meno, what matters is that both examinations rely on the same theory of knowledge and are conducted according to the same rules.

The fact that inquiry is successful in one case does not entail that it will be successful in the other. Socrates never offers a guarantee. In response to Meno, all he has to show is that inquiry is not a waste of time.

To account for the possibility of successful inquiry, Socrates resorts to the doctrine of immortality. This doctrine, if true, would mean that every respondent carries with him the knowledge of all things so that allowing the respondent to certify the truth of what is said is not as foolish as it might first appear. If a slave can be taken to the frontiers of mathematics, then in principle he is in as good a position as anyone to say when a correct solution has been found. That is why the respondent must always be treated with respect. Meno does not recognize the democratic implications of this theory nor does Socrates point them out. In any case, the connection between a religious idea like immortality and an epistemological one like knowledge is itself in need of explanation.

3. KNOWING AND REMEMBERING

Socrates' account of the examination of the slave is that he has recovered knowledge out of himself and this recovery is recollection (85d). How does the recovery of a previous piece of knowledge explain the possibility of inquiry and learning?[8] Following Julius Moravcsik, we can say that memory involves two dimensions: historical and entitative.[9] The historical has to do with the fact that what we remember is always a past event. If X remembers something, there must have been an earlier time at which she first experienced it. But the historical dimension is not enough: from the fact that X experienced something in the past, it does not follow that she can remember it in the present. Here Moravcsik introduces the entitative dimension: if X remembers something in the present, there must be an entity in her mind which is causally related both to her present experience and to her experience of the past event. Put otherwise, remembering something is not the same as thinking it twice on separate occasions. When we remember something, we are not just thinking a thought but thinking a thought which is connected to a previous experience.

The main problem in interpreting Socrates' claim that inquiry and learning are recollection is what weight to give to the historical component. What does it mean to say, as Socrates does at 86a, that the soul was always in a position of having learned its knowledge? A literal interpretation of these remarks would imply a specific time, prior to this life, when the soul first beheld (*heōrakuia*, 81c) everything it knows.[10] In other words, if we take the notion of recollection seriously, we are committed to: (a) a time when the soul originally acquired its knowledge, (b) a time when it lost or forgot it, and (c) a later time when it recovers what it once had. Obviously the soul cannot have acquired its knowledge at (a) with the same methods used to recall it at (c). One cannot solve the problem of how inquiry is possible in the present by claiming it recalls the results of inquiry conducted in the past. That only puts the problem off.[11] To offer a solution, one would have to claim that the knowledge acquired at (a) is apprehended in a unique fashion: that it was obtained in a primordial moment—perhaps, as Bluck suggests, when time began—so that the soul, assuming a disembodied state, had direct acquaintance with everything it now seeks to recall. This interpretation is supported by the use of the perfect tense at 81d and 86a: Socrates claims that the soul is forever in a state of *having* learned (*memathēkuia*) what it now seeks.[12] Since the process is completed, must there not have been a time when it originally took place? It is also supported by the myth of the *Phaedrus* (247c–248e), a passage in which Socrates describes how the soul first contemplates true reality but is prone to forget what it saw.

The literal interpretation is open to the following objection. If the soul lost its knowledge completely, the fact that it once had it will not help to explain how it can engage in inquiry in the present. To press this point, Meno would only have to rephrase his puzzle: There is no point in trying to recollect knowledge which we have not forgotten because we have not forgotten it. But neither is there any point in trying to recollect what we have forgotten because it is lost to use forever.[13] To answer this objection, a proponent of the literal interpretation would have to put more weight on the entitative component. What is forgotten is not lost forever but can be recalled with sufficient effort. It is in the mind even if one must exert herself to bring it to consciousness.

But then we are inclined to ask why the historical dimension is needed at all. The overall direction of scholarship in this century has been to "demythologize" the theory of recollection by arguing that the historical component is unnecessary. It is nothing but Plato's way of describing the feeling of familiarity one has in grasping an eternal truth, the feeling that one has found what was, in Laches' words, on the tip of the tongue. According to Ovidia Hansing:[14]

> Undoubtedly it is the feeling tone which accompanies the learning process that, in part at least, causes Socrates to refer to the latter as a cause of "recollection" and to connect it with temporal and empirical memory. When one has solved a mathematical problem, for example, one experiences a feeling of certainty, of satisfaction, almost of familiarity, which can best be expressed by the word *re*cognition. It is as if the knowledge gained is really an old friend, forgotten for a while, and again called to mind.

Surely this feeling can be explained without invoking the prior existence of the soul. Suppose the soul is endowed with innate ideas from birth. These ideas are "in" the soul even if people have not always been able to articulate them. Since they are in the soul, we have enough understanding of them to begin inquiry in an intelligent way. But on the metaphorical interpretation, there is no primordial moment in which a disembodied soul first beheld them. To say that inquiry and learning are recollection is merely to say that the job of clarifying these ideas is *a priori*. On this view, then, the theory of recollection is simply the first expression of a theory of *a priori* truth.

Is recollection nothing but a metaphor to explain the *a priori* or does it actually involve recall of something grasped at a previous time? Unfortunately Plato is not anxious to tell us what part of his theory is metaphor and what part literal truth. The argument of 85d–86d raises the questoin of whether the soul once acquired its knowledge or always had it. But the question is never resolved. Socrates wants to drive home the point that the soul has knowledge it has not acquire in *this* life. The first alternative, that the soul always had its knowledge, is raised, and then dropped; presumably because Socrates thinks it establishes his point immediately. The second alternative, that the soul once acquired its knowledge, is discussed in some detail with the addition of a crucial fact: if the slave once acquired his knowledge, it must have been in a previous existence since no one has taught him geometry (85d–e). Socrates then leaps to the conclusion that if the slave has this knowledge when he is in human form, and had it before he was in human form, he must *always* have had it (86a), in which case his soul is immortal. In this way, Socrates' argument has a neat logical structure. If the soul always had its knowledge, it has always known what it is searching for. If it acquired its knowledge in a previous life, then, again, it has always known what it is searching for.[15] Therefore it must always have known what it is searching for. Therefore it is immortal.

Since the two alternatives lead to the same conclusion, the difference between them is not very great for Socrates' purposes.[16] Both imply that the knowledge being sought is already in the soul. Therefore the soul must have knowledge, or at least true opinion, which can be brought to a conscious level by questioning. It is still possible to maintain either: (1) the soul knew these truths in a subliminal way for infinite time, or (2) it acquired them by direct acquaintance when it was in a disembodied state.

The problem with the metaphorical interpretation is, as Moravcsik points out, that virtually all of the work is done by the entitative component. However the slave first acquired his knowledge of geometry, what matters is that he can recover it for himself, that is, bring it to consciousness, *in the present*. It would seem, therefore, that we can suspend the question of how knowledge of geometry made its way into the soul and direct attention to how it is recalled. If so, it is the entitative component which answers Meno's puzzle. Moravcsik points to 85c, where Socrates claims recollection is the process of bringing to conscious knowledge that which was in people all along. Again, the question of how it got there is unimportant.

To be more specific, the entitative component answers Meno's puzzle by denying the premise on which it is based. That puzzle began by assuming an exhaustive disjunction between knowledge and ignorance: either we know something or we do not. In the first case, inquiry is superfluous; in the second, impossible. But the entitative component of remembering shows that this disjunction is false for it calls attention to a type of knowledge that is in the soul even though it is not grasped with full clarity. A person trying to recall a piece of information is not ignorant of it since it could be recovered with sufficient effort. But neither does she know it in the sense of having it directly before her mind. Socrates' point is that our knowledge of geometry exists in a similar state: it is at our disposal in the sense that proper questioning can arouse it even if we do not currently have it in mind. If this is true, then the all or nothing assumption behind Meno's puzzle is bogus and inquiry is not a waste of time.

According to the metaphorical interpretation, the purpose of recollection is to indicate that knowledge is not in the soul in the way that money is in a bank: credited or not. In addition to the knowledge directly before our minds, there is knowledge in the form of latent opinions, intuitions, or capacities.[18] The term *knowledge* is therefore ambiguous: it can refer to what is grasped with full clarity or to what is *capable* of being grasped with full clarity if one submits to *elenchus*. Socrates is talking about knowledge in the first sense at 84a–b and at 85c when he claims that the slave does *not* know the answer to the geometry problem. He uses the same sense of the word when he says at 86b that we can inquire into what we do not know. But he implies the second sense when he claims that the soul has learned all things (81c) and that the salve was forever in a state of having learned the answer to the geometry problem (85c, 86a).[19] Meno assumed that the first is the only legitimate meaning.

If the slave's knowledge has *always* been in his soul, it cannot be affected by anything peculiar to a specific incarnation. It must true in whatever state the soul finds itself. So once agian we are back to the notion that the theory of recollection is nothing but a roundabout way of providing for the possibility of *a priori* truth, in which case the relevance of immortality is still unclear.[20]

4. RECOLLECTION AND IMMORTALITY

The metaphorical interpretation answers Meno's puzzle by rejecting the either/or assumption on which it is based and calling attention to intermediate states of awareness. The existence of such intermediate states is demonstrated by the examination of the slave. Even when he gets the right answer, Socrates describes his understanding of geometry as a dream-like awareness (85c). But if intermediate states are all that is needed to answer Meno, why bring in all the material connected with the historical component?[21]

Socrates does not present this material with complete conviction. After concluding that the soul is immortal, he says to Meno that there are parts of the theory of recollection he would not swear to. It is easy to see why Plato would put such a qualification in his mouth. Since the Socrates of the *Apology* (40c–d) expressed agnosticism about life after death, claiming it was either a loss of consciousness or a migration of the soul to another place, it would not do to have the Socrates of the *Meno* affirm a specific doctrine with confidence. Thus the theory of recollection is offered as something Socrates has heard but not something to which he is completely committed. Still, if the historical component were irrelevant, Plato could have spared himself and the reader a lot of wasted effort by leaving it out. The fact that Socrates does not commit himself to everything it involves does not mean that the reader can pass over it lightly.

Here it is worth noting that Socrates' explanation for the presence of *a priori* truths in the soul is not Kant's: that they are necessary conditions for the possibility of experience. There is no mention of forms of mental activity or structures which the mind imposes on reality. Socrates' explanation of *a priori* truth is to focus on the object which the mind apprehends. Thus the claim (81c) that the mind has seen all things. The result is that with the exception of a brief and enigmatic passage in the *Phaedo*, he never considers the possibility which seems so obvious to us: that the soul is endowed with latent knowledge *at* birth rather than *before*.[22] Nearly a hundred years ago, Stock objected that: "There is no notice taken of the possible supposition that the boy got the knowledge on coming into this life, that is to say, that it is part of his human nature."[23] This objection is felt most keenly at 85d–e, when Socrates offers the fact that no one taught the slave geometry in this life as a reason for thinking that he must have known it before entering human form.

What is more, even if we grant that the soul existed before birth, Socrates' argument does not prove that it is undying (*athanatos*, 81c, 86b). Again, we are never told why a soul which will perish when this life is over cannot apprehend truths which remain valid forever. Why can truth not be immortal even if the individual soul which grasps it is destructible?

The most obvious answer is, as Norman Gulley put it, that in the *Meno* Plato is only beginning to consider the implications of his theory of knowledge.[24] One such implication is made clear at *Phaedo* 76d–e: that the existence of eternal objects of knowledge and the existence of an eternal soul stand or fall together. To quote the exact words, they have the same necessity (*hē autē annankē*). If we ask why this should be the case, we are taken back to an assumption encountered in a previous chapter: the kinship between knower and object known. Behind this assumption is the idea that knowledge requires entry into or contact with a realm of eternal objects. If the soul were unlike the objects it seeks to apprehend, such contact could not occur. According to *Phaedo* 79d:

> When the soul inquires alone by itself, it departs to the realm of the pure, the everlasting, the undying, and changeless, and being akin to it, the soul remains forever with it . . . Then it ceases from its wanderings and remains always in the same state in relation to its object, because it is contact with things to which it is similar. And this condition we call knowlege.

David Gallop compares this assumption to the Empedoclean notion that "like knows like."[25] Grote traces it back to the Pythagoreans.[26] Whatever its origins, it is central to the theory of knowledge in dialogues as diverse as the *Republic, Phaedrus,* and *Timaeus,* not to mention the *Phaedo* itself.[27] The fact that it is often mentioned in conjunction with myths or moral injunctions is no reason why it should not be taken seriously. As Bluck remarks, the general tendency of both Plato and Aristotle is to assimilate the conception of the cognizing soul to the divine objects of its cognition.[28] Even in the case of god, a divine nature requires contact with a divine object (*Phaedrus* 249c).

There is no unambiguous mention of this assumption in the *Meno* and no mention of the metaphysical dualism to which it eventually gives rise. We have seen that according to *Meno* 81d, all nature is akin. It is unclear whether this remark means: (a) all objects of knowledge are linked by relations of implication or (b) the soul is akin to what it comprehends. Gulley follows Grote in arguing for the second interpretation, but there is no decisive evidence in the *Meno* itself.[29] The immediate context—*because* all nature is akin, and the soul has learned all things, there is nothing to prevent it, having recalled one thing, to recall the rest—is compatible with either one or both.

The kinship assumption is invoked here to explain how Socrates can go from the slave's grasp of a truth not acquired in this life to the conclusion that the soul of the slave must have existed prior to this life and will continue to exist afterwards; in short, why Socrates is so anxious to assimilate a property possessed by a truth to a property possessed by the soul. According to the kinship assumption, a temporal soul would be of a different order than the object of its knowledge and thus could not appropriate it. It would be subject to forces or metaphysical constraints which would prevent it from rising above the specific features of this life.

A contemporary philosopher might object that the kinship assumption is nothing but a consequence of thinking that knowledge involves contact between the mind and its object. Of course if such contact is to occur, the mind and its object have to be similar. But is this a legitimate way of looking at knowledge? The fact is, however, that the kinship argument has had a long career in the history of philosophy. For centuries it was the standard defense of immortality.[30] Cognitive faculties are specified by their objects. Material objects are limited in space and time. Therefore if the soul can grasp an eternal truth like that grasped by Meno's slave, it cannot be material. If it is not material, it is not corruptible. Therefore the soul's ability to grasp an eternal truth is evidence of its immortality.

Again, the kinship assumption is not found in the *Meno* in unambiguous form. All the text gives us is an argument whose conclusion goes well beyond anything justified by the premises. We can dismiss the argument or we can view it as a first attempt to formulate what would soon become a well-known principle. If I am right in thinking that kinship is a hidden premise, we can understand why, despite *our* difficulties with the historical component of recollection, Plato never gave it up. If anything, he adheres to it with greater tenacity in the *Phaedo* and *Phaedrus*. According to the fully articulated version of the theory, the grasp of an eternal truth involves more than a feeling of familiarity; it implies that the soul has the same metaphysical standing as its object so that if the existence of the object is not limited in space and time, neither is the existence of the soul. Whether the soul ever enjoyed direct acquaintance with its object is unclear. The point is that if the soul is not limited in space and time, and if it did not acquire its knowledge in a particular incarnation, it must have always known it, albeit in a confused or subliminal way.

The slave's grasp of an eternal truth is thus a turning point. From here onwards, the immortality of the soul and the objects of its knowledge will be what Cornford called the twin pillars of Platonism. If the price we pay for "demythologizing" the theory is that immortality drops out, then from the standpoint of textual accuracy, the price is unacceptably high. Too many people in the history of philosophy have embraced the kinship assumption for a commentator to dismiss it as "myth." For Plato to abandon this assumption, he would have to abadon large portions of his theory of knowledge and view the relation between the mind and its object in a way unknown to anyone in his time. But even if he were to do this, Cornford would still be right: without this portion of his theory of knowledge, it is not just immortality which would fall by the wayside, but much of the impetus for the theory of forms.

5. THE DUTY TO INQUIRE

Having presented the theory of recollection and examined the slave, Socrates' conclusion is another moral injunction: that we will be better and braver if we believe it our duty to inquire into what we do not know (86b–c). What makes this injunction important is the universality of its scope. In the fifth century, Greek morality was, as Vlastos indicates, still to a large extent a class morality.[31] Those who promised to teach virtue, the sophists, directed their activities to the wealthy. Meno himself had restricted male virtue to those capable of holding power and using it to their own advantage. The significance of Socrates' examination of the slave is that in principle truth is as accessible to him as it is to his master. Thus Socrates suggests that with further questioning, the slave could have an understanding of mathematics as good as anyone's (85c). If so, the duty to inquire does not recognize class distinctions.

From the fact that truth is as accessible to the slave as it is to the master, it does not follow that everyone has an equal chance of recovering it. In the first place, there is no reason to suppose that everyone will recognize the duty to inquire, and having recognized it, there is no reason to suppose that everyone will submit gracefully to refutation. Meno has trouble on both counts. So the universal accessibility of truth is compatible with serious doubts that large numbers of people will avail themselves of it. An egalitarian epistemology need not imply an egalitarian political theory.[32] According to the *Meno* (100a), most people are no better than the shadows that move about in Hades.

The issue of individual differences leads to what may seem like another paradox: in one respect, truth is *more* accessible to the slave because there is a greater chance that he will exhibit the moral qualities needed to conduct inquiry, in particular the willingness to admit error. Because of his social status, the slave has less to lose if he is shown to be mistaken. No one expects him to get the right answer because he has not had training in geometry. Meno is a different story. He is rich, well educated, and used to speaking in front of large audiences. He thus has more invested in his answers than does a household hand. The same is true of Socrates' other respondents who are, on the whole, a privileged class. In the *Charmides*, for example, Socrates points out on two occasions that Critias is worried about his reputation (162c and 169c).

Unlike Meno, the slave has no trouble with the duty to inquire. He becomes confused, but does not blame his confusion on Socrates. He is encouraged, but does not require anything like the flattery Socrates extends to his master. When the inquiry breaks down at 84a, the slave is willing to start over again at a moment's notice.

It would appear, therefore, that Socratic inquiry is open to an objection. We have seen that its goals are twofold: to arrive at truth and relieve the false conceit of ignorance. In regard to the latter, it works best on those least in need of its benefits. Again, we are faced with the conclusion that inquiry involves a circle. To admit that one does not know and accept the duty to inquire, one must *already* possess the honesty which the elenctic process is supposed to instill.[33] That is why Meno's slave is a better respondent than his master. If one is not willing to admit that she does not know, or is not willing to admit that she has been refuted, *elenchus* cannot work. In short, just as knowledge must be in the soul for inquiry to be possible, a certain degree of virtue must be present as well.

The theory of recollection supplies an answer to the first of these concerns. It explains how knowledge is in the soul and therefore how truth can be obtained. But it does not answer the question of how an intractable person like Callicles, or Polus, or Thrasymachus can be improved by talking with Socrates. Let us recall the claim of the *Seventh Epistle* (344b), where the kinship assumption is also found: it is only when we ask and answer questions in a spirit of benevolence that discovery can take place. In this respect, the real test of *elenchus* is not the examination of Meno's slave but the examination of Meno himself.

Though a wealthy aristocrat, he is not so old or set in his ways to be beyond hope of reforming his character. As the dialogue opens, he is about 18 years old, Socrates about 70. He has studied with Gorgias, displays some familiarity with the poets, and knows enough geometry to be able to follow Socrates' examples. More important, he raises what has emerged as the key question regarding the *elenctic* process: Can virtue be taught? We have seen that the *Apology* is self-referential in the sense that Socrates exhibits the very thing he is talking about. One is therefore inclined to ask whether Meno, the person who asks about the teaching of virtue, is taught virtue in the dialogue named for him. It is to this quesiton that we must now turn.

Notes to Chapter Five

1. Julius Moravcsik calls attention to the fact that Socrates' formulation of the puzzle is not the same as Meno's; in particular, Socrates' version is broader. See ''Learning as Recollection,'' in Vlastos (ed.), *Plato*, Vol. I

(Garden City, New York: Doubleday, 1970), p. 57. But I agree with Nicholas White that whatever we may think of the difference between the two formulations, it is hard to suppose that Plato would have Socrates respond to something Meno had not asked. Thus Socrates' reformulation is supposed to get to the kernel of Meno's question even though the wording is somewhat different. See White, *Plato On Knowledge and Reality* (Indianapolis: Hackett, 1976), 56. On the other hand, my overall interpretation is much closer to Moravcsik than to White.

2. R. S. Bluck, *Plato's Meno* (Cambridge: University Press, 1964), 297.
3. For this insight, I am indebted to R. E. Allen.
4. For further discussion, see Moravscik, *op. cit.*, 61–9.
5. In an important article, Malcolm Brown claims that the boy's success is not unqualified any more than Meno's is. The reason is that both inquiries are conducted improperly: at an important point, they put off the prior question (*ti esti*) and ask a posterior one (*poion ti*). Brown is certainly right about the discussion with Meno. But is he right about the one with the slave? According to Brown, an important shift occurs when Socrates moves from asking an arithmetical question to asking for a geometrical one. Arithmetic was, for Plato, a rigorous inquiry but unfortunately one which could not answer the question Socrates has posed. Geometry could furnish an answer but, Brown contends, at the cost of rigor. In Brown's defense, there is no question that Plato had doubts about the philosophical foundations of geometry. Those scholars who think he is using it as a model of inquiry are missing a number of points. But are these points at issue in the current passage? Here Brown is less convincing. The use of *poion* at 84a may or may not indicate that the inquiry is now being conducted in a less rigorous way. Similar considerations apply to Brown's remarks about the introduction of "causal language" (*gignontai*, 85a) and other subtle changes in expression. Plato does want to criticize geometry on the ground that it pus the *poion ti* questions first, e.g. *Republic* 533–534. But I think Brown is straining to find all of these criticisms here. See "Plato Disapproves of the Slave-Boy's Answer," *Review of Metaphysics* 20 (2967), 57–93.
6. Vlastos, "Anamnesis in the *Meno*," *op. cit.*, 159–60. Again, the chief problem with Vlastos' interpretation is his attempt to limit recollection to deductive inference and the perception of analytic connections. We have seen that there is no way the slave can solve the geometry problem by analysis or deduction alone. What is behind Vlastos' interpretation is the assumption that the *a priori* and the analytic are identical. This is a plausible view to attribute to a twentieth century logical positivist; but where is the evidence it should be attributed to Plato?
7. Cf. Kierkegaard, *Philosophical Fragments, op. cit.*, 22.
8. Note the conjunction at 81d: inquiry *and* learning are wholly recollection.
9. Moravcsik, *ibid.*
10. For a scholar sympathetic with this approach, see Cherniss, "The Philosophical Economy of the Theory of Forms," in Allen (ed.), *op. cit.*, 4.

11. This point is made by E. S. Thompson, *The Meno of Plato* (London: Mac-Millan, 1901), 143.

12. The perfect tense is also used at *Phaedo* 72e. But how can we maintain there was a specific time when the soul first beheld its knowledge if Socrates claims that the soul always (*aei*) had it? (86a: " . . . his soul is through all time in a state of having learned?" and 86b: " . . . the truth of things that are is always in the soul . . . ") The answer is that if there was a specific time when the soul first beheld its knowledge, this time would have to be either the first instant of creation or an atemporal state prior to creation. For further discussion, see Bluck, *op. cit.*, 316-7.

13. Cf. Nicholas White, "Inquiry," *Review of Metaphysics* 28 (1974), 305.

14. Ovidia Hansing, "Plato's Doctrine of Recollection," *Monist* 38 (1928), pp. 261-2. For an extreme version of the mythical interpretation, see Frutiger, *Les Mythes de Platon* (Paris: Alcan, 1930), 70-6.

15. On how the soul could *always* have known what it is searching for if it acquired its knowledge at a specific time in the past, see n. 12 above.

16. The same conclusion is reached by Klein, *op. cit.*, 179. Cf. Bluck, *op. cit.*, 313.

17. At 85c, e, 86a, Socrates claims that the slave has true opinions in his soul, while at other times he talks about truth (86a) or knowledge (81c, 85d). The point is cleared up by interpreting true opinion as *latent* knowledge. Cf. Bluck, *op. cit.*, p. 313.

18. By stressing latent knowledge, I follow in the footsteps of Cornford, *Principium Sapientiae* (Cambridge: Cambridge University Press, 1951), Chapter Four. A very different interpretation is offered by White in "Inquiry," *ibid.*, and *Plato on Knowledge and Reality, op. cit.*, Chapter Two. For White, inquiry is like looking for a physical object. The problem is then how we can have a specification of that object without already knowing it. How, for example, can we specify the reference of *virtue* clearly enough to begin a search without having the knowledge which the search is supposed to produce? The solution according to White has to do with reference. Thus we can specify the object of a search by saying that the candidate with the most votes will win the election without knowing who the successful candidate will be. So it is not the case that a specification of the object implies knowledge of it. For criticism of White, see Irwin, *Plato's Moral Theory, op. cit.*, 315, no. 12 and Michael Morgan, "How Does Plato Solve the Paradox of Inquiry in the *Meno*?" unpublished manuscript presented to the Society of Ancient Greek Philosophy, Chicago, 1985.

19. Cf. Aristotle, *Posterior Analytics* 71b7 ff. Failure to draw this distinction mars the account of Gregory Vlastos, "*Anamnesis* in the *Meno*", *op. cit.*, 153, no. 14. Vlastos claims that passages like 84a-b and 85c, where Socrates says that the slave does not know the answer to the problem, are incompatible with the view that his soul already has the knowledge it is

seeking. Accordingly, he must weaken the sense of *having learned* at 81d and 86a and interpret Socrates as saying only that all people have (i) some (but not all) knowledge, (ii) the ability to see logical relations, and therefore (iii) the ability to extend their knowledge. But what Socrates actually says at 85d and again at 86a is much stronger: that what is present in the soul is knowledge or truth, not merely the ability to grasp logical relations. The appearance of incompatibility vanishes once we recognize that he is not always using "know" in the strict sense of "to render an account."

20. On the issue of *a priori* truth, note that Socrates claims (85e) that what is true of mathematics is true of all other branches of knowledge. Still, it can be doubted whether Socratic *elenchus* can be limited to a particular class of propositions. Socrates' frequent use of analogy or myth suggests it cannot. More to the point, the dialogues are studded with social commentary, references to specific people, or other information peculiar to this life. In the *Meno* alone, Socrates offers his failure to find a successful teacher of virtue in Athens as a reason for thinking that virtue is unteachable (89d). Others have pointed out that the slave makes use of diagrams to assist in the process of recollection. The answer to this problem is that while the truths apprehended by recollection are *a priori*, the heuristic devices which help us recall them need not be. Socrates makes this point at *Phaedo* 76a, a passage whose connection to the *Meno* is explicitly remarked (73a–b).

21. Irwin, *op. cit.*, 139, suggests that all Socrates needs to answer Meno is the notion of true belief. While there is a vague reference to true belief at 85c, this idea is not introduced in a formal way until 97b. If Plato thought true belief is all that is needed, why did he approach the subject in such a roundabout way? As far as 85c is concerned, notice that the existence of true beliefs in the soul would still raise the question of their origin. If they were not imparted by others, would we not have to invoke the historical component to explain their presence? For further criticism of Irwin, see Morgan, *ibid*.

22. *Phaedo* 76d. In this passage Socrates argues that we could not acquire our knowledge at birth because that is the time we lose or forget it. In other words, since we do not have fully articulated knowledge at birth, there must be a time when the knowledge we possessed before birth is partially erased. As far as I can see, Socrates never considers the possibility that knowledge enters the soul already in a confused or indistinct form.

23. St. G. Stock, *The Meno of Plato* (Oxford: Clarendon Press, 1887), 21–22.

24. Norman Gulley, *Plato's Theory of Knowledge* (London: Methuen, 1962), 22.

25. David Gallop, *Plato: Phaedo* (Oxford: Clarendon Press, 1975), p. 140. For the reference to Empedocles, see Diels and Krantz, 31. A. 86, B9.

26. Grote, *Plato and the Other Companions of Socrates* (London: J. Murray, 1867), 17–8. For the reference to Pythagoreans, see Diels and Krantz, 14. 8a.

27. *Republic* 486d, 487a, 500c–d, *Phaedrus* 247c–d, 248b, 250c, *Timaeus* 37a–b. For discussion of the *Timaeus* passage, see Hansing, *op. cit.*, 239–140.
28. F. S. Bluck, *Plato's Phaedo* (London: Routledge & Kegan Paul, 1955), 32. According to Aristotle (*De Anima* 425b25–31, 430a2–9, and *Metaphysics* 1072b21–23), the knower, the object known, and the act of knowing it are the same. This theory was accepted by Maimonides (*Guide for the Perplexed* 1. 68) and Spinoza (*Ethics* 2.7).
29. Gulley, *op. cit.*, 9; Grote, *ibid.*
30. See, for example, Augustine, *On the Immorality of the Soul*, Chapters 1–6. Notice, however, that for the purposes of a Christian philosopher, the argument is too strong: in addition to showing that the soul will survive death, it shows that it existed before birth. Grote, *ibid.*, finds the doctrine clearly formulated in Leibniz. For a modern defense, see Joseph Owens, *An Elementary Christian Metaphysics* (Milwaukee: Bruce Publishing Co., 1963), pp. 318–20, 323–6. But Owens, too, tries to limit its scope to survival after death. According to Richard Rorty, *op. cit.*, 53, no. 23, the same argument can also be found in Descartes.
31. "The Paradox of Socrates," *op. cit.*, 19.
32. This issue is taken up by Kraut, *op. cit.*, 203–7. Against Popper, Kraut argues that nothing of moral significance is proved by the fact that Meno's slave is able to grasp a mathematical truth. This is too strong. The theory of recollection states that the soul has seen *all* things (81c) and generalizes from mathematics to every branch of knowledge (85e). At no point does Socrates suggest that what is true for mathematics might not be true for virtue. Kraut is correct in saying that the theory of recollection does not imply an egalitarian political theory. But concerning moral matters, it does imply that every soul is a repository of truth, that every soul has a duty to inquire, and that every life must be lived in the utmost holiness (81b). This is a far cry from Meno's view about the importance of wealth, power, and social class.
33. A similar conclusion is reached by Schmid, *op. cit.* He is here following Myles Burnyeat, "Socratic Midwifery, Platonic Inspiration," *Bulletin of the Institute of Classical Studies of the University of London* 24 (1977), 12.

Chapter Six
Socrates and the Teaching of Virtue

T HE *MENO* GETS GOING in a hurry. The title character, a young Thessalian aristocrat, asks Socrates whether virtue (*aretē*) can be taught.[1] Socrates' reply is full of irony. He claims that the Thessalians were once famous for wealth and horsemanship but that their fame now extends to wisdom. In Athens, he continues, it is just the opposite: there is a dearth of wisdom and so far from knowing whether virtue can be taught, the average citizen will say that he has no idea what virtue is. We are inclined to ask how Thessaly, a place whose primary interests are acquiring money and racing horses, a place which rolled out the red carpet for Gorgias, could develop a reputation for wisdom. The answer is that it cannot. In the *Crito* (53d), Socrates describes Thessaly as the home of license and disorder. And if it is true, as Socrates claims, that there is a dearth of wisdom in Athens, the appreciation of his remark requires a level of sophistication far beyond what Meno could be expected to have. The early dialogues offer ample evidence that like everyone else, the Athenians were willing to talk about virtue without bothering to ask what it is.

In any case, Meno is the perfect person to raise a question about the acquisition of virtue. Young, wealthy, headstrong, he would have been regarded by his contemporaries as the sort of person who would some day make a name for himself. Various comments in the dialogue indicate that he is handsome and used to getting his way (e.g., 76a–b). Though he was not more than twenty when he left Athens, he was put in charge of over a thousand Greek mercenaries fighting on behalf of Cyrus. Why was a young man given such sweeping responsibility? According to Bluck: " . . . a young man of rank and impetuous nature might well seem to the adventurous Cyrus well fitted to be a commander."[2]

117

Xenophon, in the *Anabasis*, portrays Meno as vicious, greedy, and disloyal.[3] Part of the reason for this may be that Xenophon was himself a close friend of Meno's arch rival, Clearchus. At any rate, Meno was accused of double dealing after the death of Cyrus and executed. Plato's portrait is not as critical and there is a good reason why. To present Meno as a moral idiot or as someone whose nature is inherently corrupt would beg the central issue: the teaching of virtue. For if some people are bad by nature, teaching, practice, or anything else would be a waste of time. It is hardly surprising, though, that scholars have disagreed on Meno's portrayal in the dialogue. Klein, who is strongly influenced by Xenophon, emphasizes Meno's incorrigibility.[4] Brumbaugh, who calls attention to the salutary effects of Socratic questioning, emphasizes his improvement from one section of the dialogue to another.[5]

The truth is that Plato has gone out of his way to present a *balanced* picture. Though Meno enjoys the privileges which come with high birth and good looks, there is no trace of meanness or treachery. Unlike Polus or Thrasymachus, he does not hurl insults at Socrates, and unlike Callicles, says nothing very shocking. In fact, his views are typical of his time. He associates male virtue with competent management of the affairs of the city—precisely the thing Protagoras claimed to teach when he promised to make his students better men (*Protagoras* 319a). Meno thinks that silver, gold, and high office constitute the good things in life. With prodding from Socrates, he agrees that they must be acquired in a just and temperate way, but has to be reminded of this agreement twice (73d, 78d). His forgetfulness suggests that he is not clear on the relation between external goods like money and influence and the character of the person who acquires them. It may be argued, however, that his lack of clarity on this point is fairly common. In the *Republic* (362–3, 366e), Adeimantus points out that people praise justice only for the reputation, honors, and rewards which follow from it.

There is, however, no reason to think that in asking how virtue is acquired, Meno is anything but sincere. The Greek word *aretē* is a noun corresponding to the adjective *agathos* as "goodness" corresponds to "good." It is as strong a word of praise as Greek possesses.[6] Thus the question "Can virtue be taught?" really amounts to the question "Can people be taught how to live a successful life?" It is clear that in the manner in which Mano has asked it, the question begs a number of issues. In the first place, Meno does not say very much about the sort of teaching he has in mind. He distinguishes teaching from practice (*askesis*), but in the absence of a prevailing educational philosophy, *teach* might mean anything from memorization to imitation or from military training to the sort of thing one finds in a finishing school. If there is a problem about teaching, there is also one about virtue or excellence. One's opinion on the teaching of virtue is likely to differ depending on whether "virtue" involves making a name in the proper circles or respecting the rights of others. As noted above, Meno is never quite sure whether virtue or excellence is to be interpreted in a moral or a strictly prudential sense. In fact, he may not have been clear on the difference. In either case, the question "Can virtue be taught?" cannot be answered directly. One must first determine what the subject of the question is. There may be people who can inculcate the qualities needed to achieve wealth and influence. But can someone actually teach another how to act in a just and temperative way?

1. PROTAGORAS AND GORGIAS ON MORAL IMPROVEMENT

These sort of issues were very much on the mind of fifth century Greeks. In the dialogue which bears his name, Protagoras claims that if someone becomes his pupil, "On the day you begin, you will return home the better for it, the same will be true next day, and each and every day will contribute to your improvement" (318a). In the *Meno* (91d ff.), Socrates claims that Protagoras was in the business of teaching virtue for over forty years and amassed a fortune. This fact is all the more remarkable when one considers that Protagoras is said to have allowed his students the privilege of *not* paying tuition if they found no value in his courses (Diels and Krantz, A6). Yet the precise nature of his teahcing remains something of a mystery. According to the Protagoras who appears in Plato's dialogue, virtue is the one thing without which a society cannot exist (*Protagoras* 324d). Therefore the job of teaching virtue belongs to society at large. To ask "Who teaches virtue?" is like asking "Who teaches Greek?" We all rebuke our neighbor for doing something wrong and praise her for doing something right. All Protagoras does is to facilitate this process, to "lead the way" to virtue (328b).

But in leading the way, does he offer himself as a friend of traditional values or a critic? The "Great Speech" shows us one face, but his frequent attacks on the opinions of the many (317a, 333c, 352e,

353a) and his professed agnosticism present another. In the *Meno*,
Anytus, who as a democratic politican could be said to represent the
view of common people, has no doubt that the sophists are a threat to
traditional values and wants them run out of town (90c). According to
some accounts (Diels and Krantz, A3, 12, 23) this is exactly what happened to Protagoras.

Meno indicates that Gorgias was more modest than Protagoras—
that he laughed at those who promised to teach virtue and thought of
himself merely as training clever speakers (95c). In the *Gorgias*,
however, Plato has the great orator say that if a student came to him
ignorant of right and wrong, he would teach him that in addition to
rhetoric. Not only does this admission conflict with the view that
Gorgias limited his efforts to training clever speakers, it conflicts with
a view Gorgias expresses earlier in the same dialogue: that like a boxing instructor, a teacher of rhetoric cannot be held responsible if one
of his students misuses the skill he has acquired (456c ff.). There is no
hope of reconstructing the position of the historical Gorgias. What is
of interest is that Plato *portrays* him as equivocating on the subject of
virtue, and that equivocation helps us to understand the problems
Meno encounters.

If virtue is the most important quality a person can have, it would
be odd for a high-priced educator to maintain that the training *he* offers has nothing to do with it. In fact, Plato has Gorgias say that
speaking ability is not just a good thing to get but the secret to a rich
and powerful life (*Gorgias* 452e). Not only can he answer questions on
any subject at all (447c, cf. *Meno* 70b), he can persuade the Assembly
to follow his advice even when he knows less about the issue under
discussion than his opponent (456c). According to his disciple, this
ability confers unique privileges on the rhetorician and enables him to
treat everyone else as a slave (466ff.). In fact it is misleading to think
of Gorgias merely as a teacher of rhetoric. As Dodds points out, people like Meno and Callicles did not pay large sums of money to learn
the intricacies of style.[7] They saw rhetoric as the means of acquiring
political power. There is something lost, therefore, when the Greek
word *rhētor* is translated "rhetorician." Since Gorgias uses this word
to describe Pericles and Themistocles (456a), it clearly means someone who addresses the Assembly on important matters, someone
whose opinions carry weight.

Why, then, should Gorgias deny that he teaches virtue? He obviously teaches the sort of thing Meno identifies with virtue when

asked to say how he *and* Gorgias define it (71d). The answer is that Gorgias is caught up in a cross current and cannot extricate himself. He more than anyone else is aware of the power of the spoken word.[8] If virtue is nothing but the ability to gain wealth and influence, then there is no one better able to teach it than Gorgias. Still, he is no Callicles and has enough scruples to say that he wants his students to use their ability in the right way. He is afraid that by denying this, he, too, will be run out of town. But how did he insure that his students would not misuse their talent? What steps did he take to guarantee that they would not speak in behalf of unworthy causes?

There is nothing to indicate that he took any steps at all. The best guess is that he taught techniques of persuasion in a morally neutral fashion. As we saw in a previous chapter, his particular type of persuasion was indifferent to truth. If this interpretation is right, Meno is not denying that Gorgias claimed to teach virtue but pointing out that Gorgias preferred to duck the question.[9] It is not surprising, then, that having studied with Gorgias, Meno is not sure whether virtue can be taught and decides to turn to Socrates for help. So understood, Gorgias' position is not only equivocal, it is morally objectionable in its own right. Again from Dodds: " . . . in Plato's view no society can afford to be content with a morally neutral education, which puts the instruments of domination into the hands of the morally ignorant."[10] But this raises Meno's question all over again: What steps should a society take to see that its citizens are morally intelligent?

2. SOCRATIC DOUBTS ABOUT THE TEACHING OF VIRTUE

Socrates was skeptical about the teachings of virtue—or at least about the people in the fifth century who promised to do it. In the *Apology* (20a–c), he questions whether anyone else can teach virtue for a fee. His doubt is supported by argument in the *Protagoras* (319a ff.). According to that argument, the Athenians are wise people. When the seek advice on technical matters like shipbuilding, they enlist the service of experts. But when questions of national policy arise, they allow anyone to speak. The conclusion is that there are no experts on virtue because otherwise the Athenians would seek them out. And if there are no experts on a subject, how can it be taught?

This argument is reminiscent of one Socrates presents in the *Meno*. Here the claim that virtue can be taught is derived from the claim that virtue is a kind of knowledge. The latter claim is derived, with a fair amount of argument, from the claim that virtue is good. Yet no sooner do Socrates and Meno conclude that virtue can be taught than Socrates expresses doubts. If virtue can be taught, why, despite considerable effort, has he been unable to find someone who teaches it? Most commentators have not been impressed with this argument and it is easy to see why. From the fact that a subject is not being taught, it does not follow that it is unteachable. Calculus was not being taught in the fifth century, but no one would have been justified in concluding that it could not be taught in the future. It has even been suggested that Socrates' argument is intentionally fallacious.[11]

The truth is, however, that Socrates devotes too much time to this argument for a commentator to reject it out of hand. If calculus was not taught in the fifth century, it is because no one had any idea what it is. Not so with virtue. Virtue was on everyone's mind, and there is an obvious respect in which everyone tried to teach it or learn it. The thrust of Socrates' argument is that if virtue is not being taught, it is hardly for lack of effort. The wealthiest and most talented men in Athens have gone to great lengths to teach it to their sons.

In fact, Socrates' argument does not require him to hold that the absence of teachers of virtue *entails* that it cannot be taught—only that it provides strong reason to think so. Consider an analogy offered by Richard Kraut.[12] Suppose our present theories lead us to conclude that a certain metal can be shattered. Yet suppose that after numerous and elaborate attempts to shatter it, nothing has happened. One could argue that the metal *can* be shattered but that we have not gone about it in the right way. But it is hardly fallacious for someone to conclude that the metal cannot be shattered and therefore the theories which say otherwise must be revised. So while the absence of teachers of virtue does not show positively that virtue cannot be taught, it casts considerable doubt on this claim and shifts the burden of proof to those who think it can. Clearly virtue is the single most important thing a person can have. Thus it is reasonable for Socrates to suppose that if virtue were teach*able*, someone would be teaching it— if not to strangers, then at least to his own children (cf. 93c). And if in a city that produced Herodotus, Thucydides, Aeschylus, Sophocles, Euripides, Phidias, and the like, no one has arisen to teach it, it does begin to seem that virtue is not like other subjects.

Bluck tried to weaken the force of Socrates' argument by pointing out that Socrates is talking about only *such virtue as exists at present*:[13]

> Socrates does not argue from the absence of teachers of virtue both now and in the past to the conclusion that virtue cannot

ever be taught; his 'not teachable' means simply 'not teachable *now*', as is shown by his allowing that one day someone might teach it.

There is an important respect in which Bluck is right. The virtue of political leaders like Pericles is not based on knowledge but on right opinion. Now since right opinion is not taught (*Meno* 99b), it follows that such virtue as exists at present is not taught. But this cannot be all that Scorates wants to say. Neither is *real* virtue taught at present. And if it has not been taught in the past or present, we have no reason to think, unless someone can show otherwise, that it will taught in the future. One can always maintain that the future will be different. Yet unless she can produce a philosophic reason why it will, Socrates has not been refuted.

If Socrates is right, if virtue is not taught at present and there is reason to think that it is unteachable, where should a person like Meno turn if he wants to improve the character of his soul? If neither the sophists, nor the poets, nor the statesmen of Athens have devised a reliable way of transmitting excellence, what is a person to do? This takes us back to the beginning of the dialogue.

3. MENO'S NEED FOR VIRTUE AND THE THERAPEUTIC EFFECTS OF ELENCHUS

The abruptness of Meno's question indicates something more about the sort of training he received at the hands of Gorgias. Without any introduction, definition of terms, consideration of examples, or citing of texts, he rushes up to Socrates and asks for an immediate answer to one of the most troublesome questions of the day. Undoubtedly he is seeking a short, high-sounding answer which, in Hegel's words, would be shot out of a pistol (cf. 76e). Such an answer could be committed to memory and retrieved at an appropriate time. Thus Meno's first definition of virtue sounds a lot like the opening lines of Gorgias' *Helen*. After that definition is rejected, he proceeds to quote an unnamed poet (77b). In practically every case, his definitions fail because he identifies virtue with a morally neutral quality like the ability to manage or the ability to acquire "fine" things. When Socrates asks him whether these activities must be pursued in a just or temerate way, he agrees that they must but then finds himself in the position of defining the whole in terms of its parts (79a ff.).

Throughout the opening pages of the dialogue, the picture which emerges is that of a pampered youth who has little patience with

Socratic questioning. At 75b, Socrates agrees to define figure if Meno will then define virtue. But when a definition of figure is finally reached at 76a, Meno is not yet willing to uphold his end of the agreement and insists that Socrates define color. Socrates replies that Meno is shameless (*hubristēs*, 76a) and behaving like a spoiled child, but gives in to keep the discussion going. Indeed, the whole interchange from 73c to 77b casts Meno in an unflattering light. Socrates first defines figure as the only thing which always accompanies color. Meno, however, replies that it is foolish to define figure in terms of color if the nature of color is also unclear.

Is it unclear? Meno did not object when color was brought into the discussion at 74c. Nor does he object later on when Socrates introduces surface (76a) and sight (76d). Why, then, does he take issue with color at 75c? It would appear that he is trying to save face. Having watched Socrates take apart his definitions of virtue, he tries to do the same with Socrates' definition of figure. In the abstract, his objection is sound. One cannot define X in terms of Y if it happens that Y is also obscure. However it is significant that Meno does not press his objection in the one place in the dialogue where it is needed. At 87b, Socrates begins to establish a connection between virtue and knowledge. Here Meno should point out that the latter term is no less disputed than the former. But instead he goes along with Socrates, indicating that his present objection is made in a spirit of contentiousness (cf. 75c).[14]

As for the definition of color, we have seen that Socrates yields to Meno. In so doing, he produces a pompous-sounding formula which has little or no explanatory power: "Color is an effluence of figures commensurate with sight and perceptible" (76d). But Meno, who rejeted Socrates' first definition of figure because it introduced unfamiliar terminology, approves of the definition of color, calling it first-rate.

Unable to put off Socrates any longer, Meno defines virtue by citing a vague formula containing a highly ambiguous term: virtue is desire for "fine" things and the ability to obtain them. When the first part of this definition is shown to be superfluous and the second part clarified, Meno's claim amounts to this: virtue is the ability to obtain-things like silver, gold, and high office. Once again, he agrees that they must be obtained in a just way, and Socrates points out that it is Meno who is attempting to define something by introducing unfamiliar terms (79d). Trapped by his own admissions, Meno decides that the fault lies not with him but with Socrates. In a blast of intemperance, he accuses Socrates of casting a spell over him and making it impossible to speak. The truth is, however, that Socrates has only reminded him of his own admissions and so far from casting a spell, has done everything possible to encourage Meno to talk.

Yet, Meno, whose laziness is hinted at in Socrates' speech of 76a–b, comes up with the paradox designed to show that inquiry is a waste of time. No doubt, he heard the paradox from someone else and is again repeating the words of another person. The paradox, if true, would enable Meno to make peace with laziness because it would abolish the need to respond to Socrates. If inquiry is a waste of time, he might just as well return to Thessaly and train horses. But the examination of the slave convinces him that inquiry is not a waste of time so that by 86c, they are ready to take up the definition of virtue once again. Though Meno's behavior has been less than admirable, Socrates puts out a helping hand: they will inquire into the nature of virtue *together*. Unfortunately Meno still insists on having things his way. Instead of returning to the nature of virtue, he demands that they take up the question of how it is acquired—thus ignoring everything Socrates and he agreed to about the priority of *ti* to *poion ti*. Socrates gives in once again and claims that Meno is completely out of control: "You don't even attempt to govern yourself" (86d).

This passage represents a turning point for two reasons. First, the definition of virtue is never again pursued in a systematic way. Although Socrates and Meno appear to make progress on the question of how it is acquired, that progress proves to be short-lived. By the end of the dialogue (100b), Socrates maintains they will never achieve certainty on these issues until they first determine what virtue is. Second, from the moment Socrates proclaims that Meno is out of control, Meno undergoes a change. He becomes interested in the issues and no longer requires inducements to continue talking. At 89d and again at 97d, it is his curiosity which moves the discussion forward. He becomes receptive to new ways of thinking. Though Anytus is outraged at Socrates' criticisms of contemporary society, Meno is not. At 96d, he wonders aloud whether there are any virtuous men, and if so, how they go that way. In general, he loses the overbearing quality which gave the early pages of the dialogue so sharp a tone. What happened?

The answer has to be that if the elenctic process had a salutary effect on the slave (84a–c), it has had a salutary effect on Meno too.[15] The person who was given the confidence to answer any question put to him (70b–c) has lost that confidence and acquired instead a thirst for inquiry. At 95c, he admits ignorance without being forced to do so. He is, then, a classic example of the therapeutic effects of *elenchus*. In the *Sophist* (229e–230e), Socrates compares *elenchus* to other types of moral education and finds it superior.

STRANGER:	Of teaching in arguments, one method appears to be rougher, another smoother.
THEAETETUS:	How are we to distinguish the two?
STR.:	There is the time-honored method which our fathers often practised toward their sons, and which many still use today: either of angrily reproving their errors or of gently exhorting them. This method as a whole may be correctly termed *admonition*.
THT.:	True.
STR.:	But some appear to have arrived at the conclusion that all ignorance is involuntary, and that no one who thinks himself wise is willing to learn the things in which he regards himself so. It follows that the admonitory sort of education gives much trouble and does little good.
THT.:	They are quite right.
STR.:	So they try to eradicate this conceit in another way.
THT.:	What?
STR.:	They question someone when he thinks he is making sense but really isn't. They easily show that such opinions are like those of people who wander. In their discussions, they collect these opinions, and placing them side by side, show they contradict one another. . . Seeing this, the subject becomes angry with himself and gentle toward others. In this way, he is relieved of the inflated and severe opinions he has of himself. This process is quite pleasant to the listeners, but produces the most lasting benefit on the subject himself. For just as physicians believe that the body will receive no benefit from food until the internal obstacles have been removed, so the purifier of the soul believes that his patient will receive no benefit from the application of knowledge until he is

	refuted, and by being refuted, is made to feel shame. He must be purged of the opinions which obstruct knowledge so he will think he knows only what he in fact knows, no more.
THT.:	This is certainly the best and wisest state of mind.
STR.:	For all these reasons, we must admit that refutation is the greatest and most proper purification. He who has not been refuted, though he be the great King himself, is in an awful state of impurity. He is ignorant and deformed in those things in which he who would be truly happy ought to be fairest and purest.

Clearly Meno has become "gentle towards others." His newly found temperance stands in contrast to the anger of Anytus and calls to mind three passages: (1) the *Crito*, where *elenchus* has a soothing effect on the title character, (2) the end of *Republic* I, where Thrasymachus becomes gentle towards Socrates, and (3) *Theaetetus* 210c, where Socrates tells his respondent he will be "gentler and more aggreeable" for having submitted to questioning. If, as Brumbaugh suggests, courage reveals itself in willingness to accept the risks of inquiry, justice in a fair sharing of criticism, wisdom in admitting what one does not know, Meno has improved on all three counts. He has come to embody, if only for a limited time, the virtues which make conversation possible.

4. VIRTUE, TEACHING, AND RECOLLECTION

Socratic questioning has made a difference in Meno's behavior. The obvious conclusion is that virtue can be taught because Socrates is here teaching it—not that he has delivered a lecture on how to make friends and influence people but that he has relieved Meno of the false conceit which money, good looks, and a stretch with Gorgias created. And in relieving him of this conceit, Socrates has helped to make him a better person. We are inclined to say that the answer to the question "Can virtue be taught?" is no if by *teach* one means the sort of activity which Gorgias, Protagoras, and the statesmen of Athens engaged in. Thus the reason Socrates and Meno reach a negative conclusion about the teaching of virtue is that they are still thinking about teaching as a process of passing knowledge from one person to another (93b). According to Cornford, the real conclusion of the dialogue is never stated but clearly implied: although virtue cannot be taught, it can be recollected.[16] The master of facilitating recollection is of course Socrates. Hence there can be little doubt that when the *Meno* claims that a person who could teach virtue would be among the living what Teiresias was among the dead (100a), it has Socrates in mind.

But the claim that virtue can be recollected must itself be expanded to capture the full significance of Socrates' discussion with Meno. The account of recollection at 81c–e implies that the essence of virtue is already known to us so that there is nothing which prevents us from discovering it. We have seen, however, that the process of recollection involves more than an isolated act of mental vision. In order to obtain that vision, one must engage in conversation, and in order to engage in conversation, she must exemplify the virtues which make it possible. So to claim that virtue can be recollected is to claim both: (1) that a person who is conceited or overbearing can be brought to a state where she is gentle toward others, and (2) that if she has become gentle toward others, she can be led to discover the essence of virtue. Can Socrates do all of this?

It is here that the conclusion "Virtue can be recollected" loses some of its attractiveness. Suppose we extend the meaning of *teach* to include Socratic questioning. The issue then becomes: must a person be successful in order to qualify as a teacher? In the *Meno*, Socrates uses the failure of the Athenian statesmen to transmit virtue to their sons as evidence that they did not teach it. The same view seems to be at stake in Socrates' refutation of Gorgias. If Gorgias would teach right and wrong to a student ignorant of them—if under these circumstances, he would attempt to teach virtue—then he must be held to account if his student's behavior leaves something to be desired. After all, we would not consider someone a teacher of medicine if his students never succeeded in curing a patient. But if these arguments apply to everyone else, why should they not apply to Socrates? If he teaches virtue in any sense of *teach*, why should he not be held responsible for the actions of Critias, Alcibiades, and the others? And why should the inconclusive nature of the *Meno* and other dialogues of search not count as evidence that he failed in what he attempted? For if truth be told, he was no more successful in turning out virtuous disciples than were the people he criticizes. He has no "products" to show off, and according to the *Laches* (186b), without such products, he has no real claim to being a teacher.

There is of course one big difference between Socrates and the people he criticizes: Socrates never *promised* that he could turn out virtuous disciples. What the theory of recollection gives us is the *hope* that virtue will be discovered and that, in the process, the respondent will become a better person. It is a long way from Socrates' offer of hope to Protagoras' guarantee that on the very day one begins his course of study he will return a better man. In short, the shift from "Virtue can be taught" to "Virtue can be recollected" is more than a semantic refinement because the latter implies what the former apparently did not: reduced expectations about the chance of success.

If it is asked why recollection has to have reduced expectations about the chance of success, the answer is that it is unlike the teaching of medicine, boxing, flute playing, or any other practical art. One can guarantee at least limited success in flute playing because the student does not have to reform his character to learn how to play a simple tune. But the whole point of recollection is that such reform *is* necessary because unlike flute playing, the respondent must continually confront his own ignorance. What guarantee do we have that when a respondent is brought to shame, he will admit his mistake rather than take out after Socrates or run away? Obviously there is none. So despite all the claims Socrates makes about the salutary effects of *elenchus*, he is understandably cautious about promising success. The question of whether the respondent will reform his character is up to the respondent. All Socrates can provide is the opportunity. If the respondent submits to the rigors of *elenchus*, he will emerge a better person. But if he refuses to submit, or submits halfheartedly, there is nothing Socrates can do. The problem is that most people submit *before* they know what will be demanded of them and begin to change their minds when they find out.

5. DID MENO LEARN VIRTUE?

We are back to the claim that elenctic education involves a circle. The person who is already conscious of his limitations will see that *elenchus* is exactly what is needed to improve his soul and will submit without hesitation. But the person most in need of it, the person who has little or no knowledge of self, is likely to back off. Myles Burnyeat is thus correct in saying that "Socratic education can only be successful with someone like Theaetetus, who is aware of and can accept his need for it."[17] For a person unaware of this need, a person like Meno, Socratic education can have at best a temporary effect. It is here that the *Meno*, like so many other dialogues, contains an over-riding sense of tragedy. Contrary to the picture we get from Klein, the young Thessalian is not beyond hope. The elenctic process does make a difference. Still, the audience knows that the difference will be short-lived. After meeting Socrates and being given a taste of real education, Meno will head for Persia and resort to his old ways.

His imminent departure is referred to at 76e, when Socrates claims that Meno would be better able to distinguish good definitions from bad if he did not have to leave before the mysteries but could stay and be initiated. Although the immediate referent of the word "mysteries" is a religious ceremony, there can be little doubt that Socrates is also referring to philosophy: similar comparisons exist at *Phaedrus* 249b–d and *Phaedo* 69c–d and are at the core of Socrates' conception of himself as a religious hero. When Meno approaches Socrates and asks "Can Virtue be taught?" he has confronted the best example of virtue Athenian society has to offer—not a perfect example, perhaps, but a better one than Meno will find elsewhere in the city and better by far than those he has found in Thessaly. But Socrates does not look or sound like the sort of teachers Meno has known, and therefore he fails to take account of what is happening to him. At no point in the dialogue does he even consider the possibility that Socrates is the person he is looking for. When the dialogue ends, he leaves Athens without any prospect of carrying on the education he has stumbled into.

The reader cannot help but feel disappointed. If Socrates knows that *elenchus* is Meno's only hope of obtaining virtue, why does he allow Meno to leave for Persia? Why does he not use all the rhetorical skill at his disposal to persuade Meno to stay in Athens and submit to further questioning? Or, barring that, why does he not get down on his hands and knees and *beg* him to stay? There is no question that if *we* were writing the dialogue, this is exactly what we would have Socrates do. He would try to break the circle described above by putting *elenchus* aside and resort to the tricks of the radio dial preacher. But, then, we are not writing the dialogue and this is not what Plato has Socrates do. No doubt, there were people in Athens who did make these sorts of appeals, but Socrates had no confidence in them. If a person is to become aware of his need for *elenchus*, she must discover it for herself. Anything less would be tantamount to putting sight in blind eyes. Though Meno would, in fact, be better off if he recognized his need for it, neither Socrates nor anyone else can teach him that this is so. It is in this sense that the teaching of virtue is impossible.

We may argue with Socrates on the grounds that the preacher is likely to be more effective and that, in any case, one cannot stand on epistemological niceties when the life of a promising youth like Meno is at stake. Socrates' reply would be that he is just as concerned about Meno's welfare as we are, but that unlike us, he really believes what he said about the examined life.[18] To depart from *elenchus*, even if the departure is to win adherents to it, is to put the prospects for such a life in jeopardy. The *Meno*, then, is a tragedy just as much of Socrates' life was tragic. The major character does not learn virtue because he decides of his own free will to cut his education short. And the audience, or a good portion of it, comes away not quite sure that Socrates did the right thing.

The tragedy would be greatly reduced if Meno was not in some sense persuaded of the truth of Socrates' remarks. If the two characters had remained at loggerheads throughout the discussion, Meno's departure would be regrettable but not tragic. Like Callicles, Meno claims that there is something fundamentally appealing in what Socrates has said (86b & 98a cf. *Gorgias* 513c). But also like Callicles, he is never completely convinced.

Did Socrates teach virtue? The question does not admit of a simple answer. His impact on Meno and Callicles is remarkable given the time he had with them. He strove mightily to turn each of them around, using every elenctic weapon at his disposal; but in the end, no soul was saved.[19]

6. PLATONIC AFTERTHOUGHTS

The choices Meno gave Socrates at the beginning of the dialogue were there: (1) that virtue can be taught, (2) that it is acquired by practise, and (3) that it is present by nature. Later on, a fourth possibility is considered: that virtue comes by divine dispensation without understanding (99e). But this alternative, which Socrates connects with poets and soothsayers, is hardly to be taken seriously.[20] The closest the dialogue comes to a positive answer is (1), even though this conclusion is never stated in so many words. According to Cornford, the theory of recollection had given a totally new meaning to *teach* and *learn*, but the dialogue stops short of drawing out the implications.[21] Those implications are that all knowledge worthy of the name is recovered out of our own soul so that the knowledge on which true philosophic virtue depends will be gained through the elenctic process.

In the *Republic*, however, Plato suggests that the elenctic process is not enough. We are told that some people have golden constitutions and are better able to acquire virtue than others (415a, 547a). Even those who have the necessary aptitude must go through rigorous physical training to develop it. So unlike the *Meno*, the *Republic* stresses natural gifts (503, 535) as well as practise or *askēsis* (518d–e). Though moral dialectic is also a part of the guardians' training, it does not come until relatively late in life—around the age of fifty. Again, Meno could not have been more than twenty when he left Athens. To the question "How is virtue acquired?" the *Republic* seems to be saying that it is acquired by combining all three of the choices Meno offered Socrates. If so, then *elenchus* alone is insufficient. The *Meno*, on the other hand, says almost nothing about the first two choices and never implies that moral dialectic must await middle age.[22] Why the difference?

There are a lot of answers to this question ranging from a more complicated moral psychology to the introduction of the theory of forms. But a discussion of these reasons would be incomplete unless it focused on the fact that the *Republic* is more cautious about the prospects of acquiring virtue—just as the *Phaedo* is more cautious about the prospects of acquiring knowledge.[23] Plato did not despair when he wrote the dialogues of his middle period, but neither could he ignore the fact that the greatest teacher who ever lived had so little success.

Notes to Chapter Six

1. Meno's question is ambiguous because the Greek word *didakton* can mean either "is taught" or "is teachable." Unfortunately the dialogue does little to clear up the ambiguity. The argument of 89d ff. offers the absence of teachers of virtue as a reason for concluding it is not *didakton*. This argument would make sense if we took Socrates to mean "is teachable," but it would be much stronger if we took him to mean "is taught." Yet I agree with Bluck, *Plato's Meno, op. cit.*, 199–200, that 93b, 93e, and 94b are best read if we take Socrates to mean "is teachable." The opening line of the dialogues could be read either way. For the sake of uniformity, I will employ the weaker reading—"is teachable" throughout.

2. Bluck, *op cit.*, 123.

3. *Anabasis* 2. 6. 21–8.

4. Klein, *op. cit.*, 199–201. One cannot fail to be impressed by the wealth of dramatic detail Klein brings to light in his interpretation. But the dialogue, as he reads it, puts Socrates in the position of conducting an exercise in futility. No one had to be told that Meno had moral shortcomings. Why go to the trouble of writing a dialogue in which this point is made *ad nauseam* and Socrates practises *elenchus* on someone who cannot possibly learn from it? On Klein's view, Meno is "depraved," "vicious," and "totally incapable of learning." The problem is that Klein is anxious to make Plato consistent with Xenophon. But we know that Plato and Xenophon often disagree about the life of Socrates. On my view Meno is not incorrigible and the *elenchus* does make a difference—for a time. The problem is that its effect is shortlived. Klein's position is attacked by Josiah Gould, "Klein on Ethological Mimes," *Journal of Philosophy* 66 (1969), p. 253–65. But Gould goes too far in the other direction, arguing that (1) we learn very little about the respondent's character in the Socratic dialogues and (2) that there is no necessary relation between the dialogue form and philosophical content. Thus both Klein and Gould overlook the fact that Meno makes moral progress in a dialogue concerned with the teaching of virtue. In order to understand the Socratic contribution to the question ''Can virtue be taught?'' we have to take this progress into account.

5. R. S. Brumbaugh, "Plato's *Meno* as Form and Content of Secondary School Courses in Philosophy," *Teaching Philosophy* 1–2 (1975), 107–115.

6. For a detailed discussion, see Arthur Adkins, *Merit and Responsibility* (Oxford: Oxford University Press, 1960), esp. Chapter 3.

7. Dodds, *op. cit.*, 10.

8. See the *Helen* 10.

9. For a similar interpretation, see Bluck, *op. cit.*, 205–6, 390.

10. Dodds, ibid.

11. See, for example, M. Koyré, *Discovering Plato*, trans. by L. C. Rosenfeld (New York), p. 17. Koyré's contention is discussed by Bluck, *op. cit.*, pp. 22–3. According to Irwin, *Plato's Moral Theory*, *op. cit.*, 302, no. 22, Plato did not intend for us to take seriously the claim spelled out at 89d: that if anything is teachable, there ought to be teachers of it. But there is no evidence in the dialogue that Socrates is anything *but* serious about this claim. Notice, for example that it is Socrates' skepticism on the teaching of virtue which makes him revise his claim that virtue is knowledge. This revision is what gives him the opportunity to introduce right opinion, a topic which Irwin thinks is one of the main achievements of the dialogue. Teloh, *op. cit.*, 51 rejects the argument on the grounds that it is inconsistent with *Gorgias* 521d–e. But all Socrates says there is that he *attempts* to teach virtue.

12. Kraut, *op. cit.*, 290.

13. Bluck, *op. cit.*, 3.
14. Cf. Klein, *op. cit.*, 62-3.
15. On this point, I am indebted to Brumbaugh, *ibid.*
16. Cornford, *Principium Sapientiae* (Cambridge: Cambridge University Press, 1952), 60. n. 1. Cf. Teloh, *ibid.*
17. Myles Burnyeat, "Socratic Midwifery, Platonic Inspiration," *Bulletin of the Institute of Classical Studies of the University of London*, 24 (1977) 12.
18. Cf. Vlastos, "The Paradox of Socrates," *op. cit.*, 12-14.
19. The negative tone of this conclusion bears some similarity to the conclusions reached by Kraut, *op. cit.*, 294-304. I agree with Kraut that according to Socrates' own statements, e.g., *Laches* 186b, to qualify as a teacher of something, a person must be able to produce successful students. And I agree that the arguments of the *Protagoras* and *Meno* designed to show that virtue cannot be taught are to be taken seriously. I would maintain, however, that Socrates *tried* to teach virtue, had some temporary successes, but failed to achieve his goal *in the long run*. To quote Schmid, he brought people to the edge of self-knowledge. *Meno* 84b-c leaves no doubt that Socrates thought the elenctic process improves the soul of the respondent. This is consistent with: (a) his description of himself as a benefactor to the city of Athens, (b) the taming effect of *elenchus* on several characters, and (c) the description of Socrates at *Sophist* 229e-230e. In regard to the latter, Kraut is forced to say that Plato is putting a label on Socrates which does not really fit. If a person devotes his entire life to improving the moral character of his associates and achieves only modest success, it will not do to say that he is a teacher of virtue and let the matter drop. But neither will it do to say that he is not a teacher of virtue in any legitimate sense. Here is one case where either/or logic prevents us from getting to the real point: the fact that *elenchus* induces a sense of shame and could reform the respondent's character *if he would give it a chance*. The problem is that most respondents do not.
20. Socrates is sharply critical of virtue "without philosophy or understanding" at *Phaedo* 82a-b. What is more, the recipients of this divine gift, Pericles and Themistocles, are themselves held up to criticism at *Gorgias* 516e-517a, 519a-b. Surely Plato's audience would have viewed the comparison between the statesmen of Athens and a soothsayer as insulting to the former. Cf. Bluck, *op. cit.*, 368. For an opposing view, see R. Hackwworth, *Plato's Phaedrus* (Cambridge: Cambridge University Press, 1952), 149, n. 3.
21. Cornford, *op. cit.*, 60-1.
22. The possibility that virtue is present by nature is discussed at 89b and rejected. Note how similar this passage is to the moral cast system of the *Republic*.
23. Compare *Meno* 81c-e to *Phaedo* 66b-67d.

Chapter Seven
Conclusion: Virtue and Knowledge

THIS BOOK HAS PRESENTED Socrates in a particular light: as a moral reformer. He is perfectly serious when he says in the *Apology* (30a–b), that he is under an obligation to practise philosophy and persuade people to pay more attention to the welfare of their souls than to wealth, fame, and beauty. And he had no doubt what would happen if people followed his advice: as Callicles once remarked, their lives would be turned upside down.[1] To see this one has only to consider his respondents' understanding of virtue prior to questioning. Piety is a way of appeasing the gods, courage boldness in the face of danger, temperance a kind of tranquillity. In Socrates' hands, all of that changed. Virtue became a quality of soul having to do more with a person's outlook on life than with specific forms of behavior. Not only must a person do the right thing, she must be in a position to say why it is right.

The addition is important. According to Socrates, the moral tests we face as human beings are not limited to those which arise in a temple, on a battlefield, or at a feast. To be able to say why something is right, one must face the test of inquiry. If a priest or soldier should fail this test, it would follow that he does not really exemplify the virtue he thinks he does. This is the clear implication of Socrates' examination of Euthyphro and Laches. All of this is a way of saying that inquiry takes center stage in Socrates' universe. There is scarcely a page where he does not avail himself of the opportunity to exhort people to inquire. Inquiry is for him the closest thing we have to a universal good—as evidenced by the fact that he was willing to engage in it with practically anyone: children, a slave, future tyrants, even a future accuser. Few people would argue with the claim that inquiry is *a* good. But is it the chief—nay, the only—way of improving character?

135

Here Socrates' position is not as clear. Moral reformers come in all shapes and sizes: prophets, teachers, law givers, political leaders, jurists, the clergy. Not all of them would approach moral improvement in the way Socrates did. Confronted with a talented youth who was about to make a catastrophic decision, most would resort to the extreme forms of persuasion contemplated in the last chapter. We have seen, however, that Socrates explicitly rejected the kind of moral education which rests on admonition (*nouthetēsis*, *Sophist* 230a). It makes no difference to him whether such admonition is angry or gentle; it is simply the wrong way to approach someone. The right way is to recognize that if a person is about to make a catastrophic decision, he is ignorant and that all ignorance is involuntary (*akousiōn*).[2]

The usual criticism of Socrates is that he gives undue emphasis to the intellectual side of behavior. In antiquity, Aristotle objected that the Socratic understanding of behavior is at variance with plain facts.[3] In the nineteenth century, Nietzsche, taking on the rationalistic tone of almost all Greek philosophy, argued that honest things do not display their reasons in the way Socrates wants.[4] There is, he continues, something indecent about the public display of reasons: it is like constantly having to put one's cards on the table. In regard to Socrates' ability to change the lives of his respondents, Nietzsche is equally adamant: "Nothing is easier to expunge than the effect of a dialectician."

Indecent or not, the examination of reasons raises the whole question of the relation between virtue and knowledge. If it is true, as I have argued throughout this book, that *elenchus* is as much a test of character as it is a test of intellectual dexterity, the connection between virtue and knowledge is at the heart of the Socratic conception of philosophy. To the degree that Socratic philosophy makes good on its claim to improve character, a close connection between knowledge can be defended; to the degree that if fails, the assumption which underlies it is bound to appear troublesome.

1. VOLUNTARY AND INVOLUNTARY BEHAVIOR

What does it mean to say that ignorance is involuntary? This remark can only be understood in connection with Socrates' moral psychology, the crux of which is that every person desires her own happiness or well-being. This claim is accepted without argument in the *Symposium* (205a), when Diotima maintains that there is no need to ask why someone wants to be happy. The *why* question would make sense in regard to specific actions but when asked of the final end of action, it makes no sense. Except for a brief passage in the *Meno*, this position is never challenged in the early dialogues. The *Lysis* (219c ff.) underscores Diotima's point by claiming that if we choose x for the sake of y, y for the sake of z, and z for the sake of something else, the process cannot go on infinitely, there must be a final good chosen for its own sake and not for the sake of something else. In the *Euthydemus* (278e ff.), we are given some idea of what the final good is. Socrates and Clinias agree that it is pointless to ask whether everyone wishes to fare well (*eu prattein*) because it is obvious that everyone does. In the *Protagoras* (358c–d), Socrates confidently asserts that it is not in human nature to be willing to go after what one regards as evil rather than good, where *evil* and *good* refer to what is harmful or beneficial to the agent.[5]

In the *Meno* (77e–78b), it is agreed that to desire evil *knowing it to be evil* is to desire something which, when possessed, will make one miserable or unhappy. Again, we should understand *evil* to mean something harmful to the agent. But, the argument continues, no one wishes to be miserable or unhappy, from which it follows that no one desires evil knowing it to be evil. Put otherwise, all who desire evil things do so in the mistaken belief that these things are good. But then while they desire things which are in fact evil, they desire them under the description of being good so that as far as their intentions are concerned, it is really good that they want.[6] If unbeknownst to me, the medicine in my glass has too high a dosage, I desire it under the description of restoring health even though in fact it will do nothing of the kind.

On this view, desire must not be understood in a mechanical way as a blind force or urge which opposes reason. The *Gorgias* goes further than the *Meno* by arguing that *all* desire aims at the final good so that no desire can be irrational in the sense that it is opposed to the agent's opinion of how that good is to be secured.[7] Thus *Gorgias* 468b:

> SOCRATES: . . . it is in pursuit of the good that we walk when walk, believing it to be the better course of action and, on the contrary, stand still when we do so for the sake of the same thing: the good.
> POLUS: It is.
> SOC.:   And so in killing, if we kill someone, or exiling

POL.:   him, or seizing his property, we think it better for us to do what we are doing than not?

POL.:   Certainly.

SOC.:   Therefore it is for the sake of the good that all those who do these actions do them.

This passage raises the question of what happens in cases where the agent is confused about her good and desires something which, if she possessed knowledge, she would certainly avoid.

Socrates' explanation follows the lines of the person who drinks medicine thinking it will restore health when in fact it will not. The *Gorgias* passage continues:

SOC.:   . . . if a person kills someone or exiles him from the city or confiscates his property, either as a tyrant or an orator, thinking it is better for him to do so, when in fact it is worse, I presume he does what seems best, does he not?

POL.:   Yes.

SOC.:   But does he also do what he wishes—supposing it is really bad? Why do you not answer?

POL.:   No, I do not think he does what he wishes.

The immediate context of these remarks is Polus' claim that tyrants and orators are admired because they can kill or exile whomever they want. Socrates' point is that it is not really killing or exiling that the tyrant wants but that for the sake of which he does them: his good.[8] Therefore if these actions fail to contribute to that good, while he does what he wants, he does not do what he intends.

Socrates' way of expressing this point is to say that the tyrant does what seems best but not what he wishes (*bouletai*, 468c). Cornford argued that Socrates is using *wish* in a technical sense meaning the desire of the true self for its own good.[9] There are two problems with Cornford's claim: (1) Plato normally avoids technical terminology so that it is hard to argue on linguistic grounds alone that wish is distinct from ordinary desire (*epithumia*); we have seen that in the *Gorgias*, wish is not opposed to another form of desire but to what seems best to the agent,[10] and (2) the phrase "true self" is not Plato's and may contain Kantian overtones which have no place in the present context. The later Academy (*Definitions* 413c) did make *wish* a technical term, defining it as desire coupled with right reason; but this text is not an infallible guide to Plato's thought. We can reformulate Cornford's point to mean that we want more from our actions than merely what seems best. It is only if what seems best actually is so that we fulfill our intentions in undertaking the action. As Socrates makes clear at *Republic* 505d–e, no one would be satisfied with the appearance of good if he could have the reality.

These considerations are what enable Socrates to say in the *Gorgias* (467a) and *Republic* (577e) that the tyrant is powerless or destitute because he never succeeds in doing what he wishes. We can agree with Polus that from the point of view of ordinary language, these claims are monstrous (*Gorgias* 467a). The tyrant does get what he thinks he wants, which is more than can be said about most people. But these expressions are only ways of saying that a person who acts in ignorance derives no benefit from his behavior. It is in this sense that ignorance is involuntary. It is not that the agent is acting under compulsion but that his actions do not do what they are intended to. Thus no one would voluntarily chose the life of the tyrant described in *Republic* VIII. If anyone does, it is only because, like Polus, he does not know how miserable the tyrant is and is deceived by appearances.

If ignorance is involuntary, we would expect that a person who came to recognize her ignorance would do everything in her power to find out the truth. We can therefore understand Socrates' conviction that he is happy to be refuted; in fact, that it is better to be refuted than to refute someone else. Refutation releives one of the burden of a false opinion which, on this view, prevents one from doing what she wishes to do. On the other hand, if a person recognized that virtue is necessary for human happiness, then, like Socrates, she would desire virtue as strongly as most people desire wealth and fame.

2. PHILOSOPHY AS THERAPY

The involuntariness of ignorance leads to a conception of philosophy which renders it indistinguishable from therapy. By making the respondent admit ignorance, Socrates is not just helping him to say what he wants to say, but more importantly, to live as he wishes to live. Put otherwise, Socratic philosophy assumes that if the respondent is laboring under false beliefs, he cannot really be satisfied with his behavior. Such dissatisfaction is evident in Crito's restlessness at the beginning of the dialogue bearing his name as well as Phaedo's shame and self pity at the end of the dialogue bearing his.[11] The search for knowledge is therefore a way of helping the respondent come to terms with himself. Such "therapy" does not involve Socrates telling the respondent what is wrong with him. Unlike Kant, Socrates does not begin with a set of maxims the respondent is obliged to accept. The material he uses to bring about a change in the respondent's behavior are the respondent's own convictions about how to live.

We can see this most clearly in the characterization of Alcibiades. On the sufrace, he is the most enviable of men: brilliant, ambitious, good looking, charismatic. None of this, it should be added, was lost on him: he is very open about his natural gifts (e.g., *Symposium* 217a). We might expect such a person to look on Socrates as a buffoon and busy himself with more weighty matters. In one respect, this is right: according to Alcibiades, anyone who hears Socrates for the first time and listens to his endless discussions of blacksmiths, shoemakers, and other craftsmen, will regard such talk as preposterous (221e). But once he gets over the initial strangeness, the effect is quite remarkable—far more than we, or Nietzsche, might expect from a mere "dialectician.' Alcibiades compares Socrates' words to the voice of a Siren (216a), the sound of a flute (215c–e), and the bite of a snake (217e–218b). He claims he has heard Pericles and the other great orators of Athens, but no one produces the violent reactions which occur when he listens to Socrates. Tears begin to flow and his heart begins to leap. Nor is this effect unusual: "I see large numbers of people suffering the same thing" (215e).[12]

What does he learn from Socrates? Exactly what Socrates claims he teaches at *Apology* 29d–e. To continue with Alcibiades: "He forces me to admit that, lacking much, I neglect myself when I attend to politics." Martha Nussbaum writes:[13]

> The presence of Socrates makes him feel, first of all, a terrifying and painful awareness of being perceived. He wants, with part of himself, to "hold out" (216a) . . . His impulse, in service of this end, is to run away, hide, stop up his ears —orifices that can be entered, willy-nilly, by penetrating words (216a–b). But he senses at the same time that in this being seen and being spoken to, in this Siren music (216a) that rushes into his body in this person's presence, is something he deeply needs not to avoid.

He wants to run from the recognition that he neglects himself but knows, or senses, that he must not avoid it.

Alcibiades is amazed by the fact that Socrates can make him feel something no one would have expected of him: shame (216b). The reason for this emotion is not that Socrates is overbearing; it is that he has gotten Alcibiades to take a close look at himself, and Alcibiades does not like what he sees. He has enough moral knowledge to be able to recognize that he is neglecting himself but not enough to make a lasting change in his behavior. The purpose of elenctic examination, then, is to appeal to this knowledge and hope that repeated questioning will lead to a new set of convictions about how to live.

It is often claimed that the reason Socratic discussions typically fail is that Socrates has imposed unrealistic standards of success. If a theory has to answer every conceivable objection which can be raised against it, of course truth will seem elusive. This objection misses an important point. The standard for what counts as success is not an external criterion like clearness and distinctness or correspondence with reality. Socrates is not looking for a procedure by which his respondents' opinions can be made to "mirror the world." In elenctic examination, success is judged by the degree to which the respondent can abide by his own admissions, which is to say the degree to which he can examine his life without feeling ashamed.[14] In this way, he himself is the standard of success. If, after taking a close look at himself, Alcibiades liked what he saw, if, after submitting to questioning, he was satisfied with his responses and did not need to make revisions, Socrates' words would have little or no effect. If, on the other hand, Socrates' words take hold of him like the bite of a snake, it is only because Alcibiades is profoundly troubled by his beliefs and the actions which take them for granted.

Again, Socrates can make the respondent the judge of his own admissions provided that the respondent comes to the inquiry with enough moral knowledge to make questioniong worthwhile. To the relativist who claims that truth is nothing but what the mass of people think on a given subject, Socrates has a simple reply: people are not satisfied with what they think. Probe beneath the surface and you will find doubt, confusion, and the characteristic feeling of shame. This emotion would not be as gripping as Alcibiades claims unless the respondent were conscious of falling short of a moral standard—even if, like Laches, he has trouble saying what this standard is. So while it is true that Socrates attempted to go beyond current beliefs and social practices, it is not true that he led his respondents anywhere they themselves did not wish to go. The dissatisfaction they feel is the result of their own judgment on the life they are defending. If the premises of that life are found wanting, so that the life itself is exposed as a sham, the respondent stands convicted on his own terms.

3. SISYPHUS REVISITED

It will be objected that if Socrates has not imposed external standards on his respondents, and asks nothing more than satisfaction with one's own life, he has misled the respondents about the ease with which such satisfactcan be achieved. Contrary to Laches' impression, the truth about virtue is not on the tip of the tongue. Put otherwise, satisfaction is not a momentary surge of confidence that one has finally got things right. Socrates' respondents often feel this way only to learn there are many objections they have not considered. Satisfaction counts for something only if it survives repeated attempts to overthrow it. But what are the chances this will happen?

This objection takes us back to the degree to which Socratic philosophy falls short of its own goals. Plato could have presented a Socrates who was satisfied with his understanding of virtue and who had a magical effect on his respondents, a Socrates whose words produced total conversion to the life of reason. Although this Socrates might not be true to life, Plato was an artist and could be granted considerable license. Instead, he makes sure that the failures of Socratic philosophy are kept in full view of the reader. Like Callicles, most respondents are not quite convinced.

How does one assess the claims of a philosopher who says straightforwardly that success has eluded him? In the *Apology*, Socrates doubts that the program of defining the virtues will ever be completed, but we have seen that he does not have an argument to prove this. A person who came to Kant with a new demonstration of God's existence would be answered with a set of *a priori* considerations designed to show that no such proof is possible. Yet a person who came to Socrates with a new theory of virtue would be questioned in detail to see if, perhaps, she had found what Socrates was searching for. Although the ancient skeptics claimed Socrates as one of their own, this is hardly a term he would use to characterize himself.[15] He has failed to define virtue and generalizes from this failure to a statement about the inferiority of human understanding. But he does not offer his failure as a reason for abandoning the search. Kant considered future attempts to prove God's existence futile; Socrates is adamant that future attempts to define virtue must continue. In fact,

Socrates typically uses his own failure as a reason for exhorting others to take up the challenge.[16]

It is almost as if Socrates would be happy to have his assessment of human understanding proved wrong. We have seen that the *Republic* (540b–c) holds open the possibility that a person might transcend human limitations and achieve the status of a demi-god. I see no reason to think that Socrates would be anything but jubilant if such a person were to appear. He might revise his assessment of human abilities, but he could point out that at least *he* had not claimed god-like status unjustifiedly. Yet whatever this hypothetical Socrates might say, the actual Socrates is still pessimistic—at least in so far as the present life is concerned. But then it seems he does put the philosopher in a Sisyphean dilemma: he exhorts us to inquire at the same time that he insists on drastically reduced expectations about the chances that inquiry will ever be completed.

The answer to this objection takes two parts. In regard to the failure to come up with a completed theory of virtue, Socrates would reply that if the prospects for achieving such a theory are dim, we have no choice but to admit this. To repeat: he has not imposed external standards of success. If, after submitting to elenctic examination, his respondents are not satisfied with their responses, it is unfair to hold him responsible. Although many people think, like Vlastos and Nietzsche, that he has forced on them a despotic logic, the truth is that he has given them maximum freedom to say what they want and has pointed out the consequences of their own admissions.[17] The danger in making success easier to achieve is that once again we will delude ourselves into thinking we know when we do not. He is not so set in his epistemological convictions that a truly successful inquiry would be embarrassing to him, but he refuses to announce success as long as difficulties remain.

In regard to getting people to admit ignorance, he would point out that an honest failure to define virtue can still have beneficial consequences. He believes he has helped the slave even when the slave is still confused. Undoubtedly he would say the same thing about Meno, Laches, Callicles, and the others: *elenchus* has taken away the arrogance they exhibit when they think they know what they are talking about. It follows that even if there is no prospect of reaching a completed theory, and like Neurath's sailor, the respondent will have to make revisions indefinitely, there is something to be gained by continuing the process. If, as Camus insists, we must imagine Sisyphus as happy, then, for different reasons, we must imagine Socrates the same way.

4. SOCRATES' INTELLECTUALISM

Thus far we have found two respects in which Socrates may be considered an intellectualist in ethics. The first is his belief that it is impossible to desire evil knowing it to be evil so that the final end of all desire is the agent's own good. If this is true, the only way a person can desire to commit a wrong is to believe, mistakenly according to Socrates, that wrong-doing benefits one. The second is his conviction that the way to improve people's behavior is to examine their beliefs about virtue and point out where those beliefs are contradictory. Clearly these points are related: if it were possible to desire something one regarded as evil, Socrates would have no reason to think that coming to believe that wrong-doing is an evil would have a salutary effect on a person's behavior. A person would agree that wrong-doing makes one unhappy but desire it anyway. In that case, Socrates might just as well resort to admonition.

On the other hand, we must be careful with the connotations of a word like *intellectualism*. Socrates' position on the teaching of virtue is not the radical assault on common sense it is sometimes taken to be. It is *not* that a person who is ignorant of virtue will learn what it is and *then* undergo some sort of moral transformation. It is rather than by examining virtue, the transformation is going on all the time. The rejection of mistaken beliefs about virtue is not like the rejection of mistaken beliefs about the weather. One of the major contentions of this book is that the respondent's behavior is no better than his understanding of what he is doing. In the last analysis, the distinction between the moral and the intellectual side of elenctic examination is impossible to draw.

If Socrates wanted to bring about an intellectual insight into the nature of virtue, he was aware that a person would have to take *and pass* a thousand moral tests to achieve it. We have seen that a person must exhibit virtue to learn what virtue is. This culminates in Plato's claim that knowledge cannot take root in an alien nature so that without a just soul, a person cannot apprehend justice. It may be said that even the decision to submit to examination is a moral act: one can always refuse to take part.

That is why commentators who ignore the dramatic component of the dialogues present a distorted picture of Socrates' position. Without the dramatic component, a dialogue is nothing but an exchange of propositions. The respondent says one thing, Socrates refutes him, the respondent says another, and so on until the end. If these propositions are taken out of context, we cannot help but lose signt of the relation between the proposition and the person who ut-tererd it. That is, we cannot help but lose sight of the fact that the per-son has something at stake in that proposition and is putting it for-ward for a reason, usually a self-serving one. What is obscured is the degree to which the respondent must make moral decisions in order to continue talking to Socrates. It then appears that according to Socrates, all one must do is survey the logical relations between pro-positions to improve one's character.

Behind this distortion is tacit approval of Robinson's preference for the impersonal march of science. Once we drop the conversational model of inquiry and look to Euclid as the paradigm, the connection between virtue and knowledge begins to seem ridiculous. The ac-quisition of knowledge is an intellectual exercise which may or may not lead to better behavior. But if the moral dimension of inquiry no longer figures in our estimation, if it is viewed as nothing but an *ad hominem* consideration, it is *we* who are the intellectualists.

It could be argued that acquiring a proper understanding of virtue is therapeutic in the sense that if we knew what virtue is, we would no longer strive for the wrong things or make decisions in the wrong way. But Socrates' position is stronger: we are helped not only by the information we get, if, indeed, we get any, but by the very process of searching for it. The process itself requires the respondent to perform virtuous acts. There are then, important respects in which Socrates is an intellectualist. But his is not the intellectualism of a modern thinker who has depersonalized the acquisition of knowledge. The considerations which Robinson dismisses as "accidental," in par-ticular the relation between the speaker and the view he is express-ing, are essential to understanding how Socrates can say that virtue, human excellence, is to be found in the activity of asking and answer-ing questions. This does not show that a person who learns what vir-tue is will, on every occasion, do what it requires. The issue of moral weakness has not yet been discussed. What it does show is that a per-son who learns what virtue is will already have performed a substan-tial number of virtuous acts. In a sense, it is true that she will be what her knowledge makes her.[18]

5. MORAL WEAKNESS: WHAT SOCRATES CAN AND CANNOT ACCOUNT FOR

Socrates is not only committed to, he openly embraces, the claim that a person never acts contrary to her understanding of her own good.[19] The obvious objection to this claim is that sometimes, owing to pleasure, fear, or fatigue, people perform actions they sincerely regret. Nothing in Socrates' position requires him to deny that people do things they regret; what he denies is that they do things knowing, or thinking, that the overall consequences of the action are harmful to them.[20] The problem posed by behavior which the agent regrets is not the fact that it occurs but the proper way of explaining it. According to the *Protagoras*, the standard explanation is that a person's knowledge is overcome by pleasure, fear, or some other emotion. For Socrates, this explanation is impossible because even in cases where the agent is feeling pleasure or beset by fear, it is still true that she is pursuing her own advantage. We would normally reject an explanation which claims the agent did something because she saw that it would make her miserable.[21] According to Socrates, if the agent does something she regrets, it must be because of a mistake in judgment. What seems like weakness of will is, then, a case of waning or inadequate knowledge.

On the basis of *Meno* 97b ff., we can broaden Socrates' explanation to include right opinion that is not held with conviction. The problem with Socrates' notion of right opinion is that it does not refer to a single state of awareness: it includes everything from Socrates' iron clad convictions about virtue (*Meno* 98b) to the hit and miss sayings of poets and soothsayers (99b–c). In regard to the former, I take Socrates to mean that a person cannot act contrary to his opinion of what is good for him *as long as he continues to hold that opinion*.[22] But I see no reason why he cannot argue that a person can act contrary to his opinion if the opinion is not secured and apt to run away. The latter would be a plausible account of what is meant by waning knowledge.

So interpreted, Socrates' position is not at variance with obvious facts. If, for exmple, a person smokes cigarettes even though she claims to know that cigarette smoking is hazardous to her health, it is still possible to argue on Socratic principles that she must desire cigarettes under the description of something good so that the issue is one of weighing that good against competing ones. To put this in a different way, the cigarette may *be* hazardous, but it does not follow that the agent desires it *as* hazardous. The *Protagoras* advances this theory in connection with hedonism, but one could certainly hold it without maintaining that pleasure is the only good.[23] It may also be true that it is pointless to admonish a person for behavior she regrets and that the only way to correct it is to achieve a deeper understanding of its causes and consequences. In any case, such behavior would not leave Socrates speechless.

But if Socrates would not be left speechless, he still has a problem. We need not go to Euripides' *Medea* to see this; we need look no further than one of Socrates' most intimate companions: Alcibiades.[24] After claiming that Socrates forces him to admit he neglects himself, Alcibiades continues: "I cannot dispute that I ought to do what he bids me to do, but as soon as I am out of his sight, I fall victim to the worship of the crowd." This repeats a familiar pattern. If Alcibiades saw nothing of value in Socrates' words and continued to regard him as a baffoon, there would be nothing to discuss. But the facts are quite different. He cannot dispute what Socrates says. More than Meno, Callicles, or perhaps any other character in the dialogues, Alcibiades is drawn to the truth of Socrates' words and the beauty of his soul. Thomas Schmid writes: " . . . Alcibiades was brought by Socrates to the very edge of self-knowledge, because he discovered through love Socrates' soul and the values of the alternative Socratic or philosophical way of life . . . "[25] Yet after being touched so deeply, what does Alcibiades do? "I run away like a slave . . . "[26]

Alcibiades is not describing the usual case of moral weakness. The issue is not an isolated case of indulgence but to what to devote one's life: repeated indulgence or self-understanding. And Alcibiades is not an ordinary person who has trouble assessing the consequences of his choices: he is in the presence of the greatest example of the philosophic life the world has known—an example whose beauty he sees and greatly admires. Schmid concludes: " . . . the tragedy of Alcibiades was that he could not abide the ugliness and humiliation this self-image involved, so he fled from the relation back into egoism and the adoration of the crowd." Again, let us grant that Alcibiades' problem is waning or inadequate knowledge. He was brought only to the edge of self-awareness. The question then becomes: Why could Socrates not take him further?

Socrates' failure to persuade the Athenians of his innocence can be explained on the grounds that he was not used to speaking in a public forum (*Apology* 24a). He did his best to defend himself, but in the end, the jury mistook the dog for the wolf. In regard to Crito's misunderstanding of the speech, we can hardly expect a person who has no real aptitude for philosophy to keep up with Socrates. In regard to Meno, Socrates could not alter an entire personality in a single conversation. But what is the explanation for Alcibiades? We know why Socrates cannot take someone by the hand and lead him to self awareness. Self-awareness is not only an awareness *of* self, but given Socrates' view of teaching, an awareness *by* self. We also know why Socrates cannot lead Alcibiades to a science of virtue: Socrates himself had not found it. The issue is why he could not persuade Alcibiades to stop neglecting himself and choose the philosophic life. According to Socrates' own principles, this is the life Alcibiades really wishes—a claim which, in a way, Alcibiades admits. Why, then, does he resist the prospect of discovery? Why does he continually seek the worship of the crowd?

Earlier we were led to the conclusion that if a person admitted ignorance, she would do everything possible to seek knowledge. The truth is, however, that Alcibiades is afraid to take the crucial step. Like the reader, he is both attracted and repelled by the presence of Socrates. But in the end, it is the latter emotion which carries the day. He resists self-knowledge and wants to run away or close himself up. According to the *Protagoras*, the popular explanation would be that the knowledge he gains from talking with Socrates is overcome by pleasure and the fear of what he will learn. The *Phaedo* would point to the impurity of the body and the distractions it imposes on the soul. A Christian thinker could invoke an inherent tendency to sin or rebel. None of these explanations is available to the Socrates of the early dialogues. To the person who recognizes the beauty of self-knowledge but backs away, all Socrates can do is trot out the familiar arguments about the benefits of virtue. The problem is that Alcibiades has heard them all before.

Socrates does not take up the philosophical challenge Alcibiades presents, and shortly after the conclusion of Alcibiades' speech, the party is broken up. Martha Nussbaum agrees that the *Symposium* offers us a choice in which Socrates and Alcibiades compete for our souls. [27] The tragedy, in her words, *our* tragedy, is that we want to have both. We want the philosophic life exemplified by Socrates and the rational ascent which culminates in love of the good. But we also want the love of particular people in their particularity. If only we could recognize the truth in Socrates' words while continuing to admire the person of Alcibiades. But we cannot have both and that is where the *Symposium* leaves us. The question is: *why* is this situation tragic? If Socrates is right about desiring the good, why are we attracted to Alcibiades at all? Why do we feel a measure of sympathy when Alcibiades claims that, despite of love for Socrates, he wants to run away? Why not regard Alcibiades as a baffoon and throw ourselves into philosophy, making light of the humiliation which goes with it?

6. PLATO AND THE TRAGIC DIMENSION OF SOCRATIC THOUGHT

The *Republic* provides the material with which to construct an answer. Desire is not one dimensional. Because there are three distinct parts of the soul, it is possible for a person to experience inner conflicts in which one part seeks what another part regards with disdain. In the story of Leontius (*Republic* 439e), we have just such a case. It is still true that virtue is a person's primary objective and that knowledge is a necessary condition for virtue. It is still true that the primary kind of knowledge is knowledge of essence and that the way to obtain it is through elenctic discussion. But with a new moral psychology comes a new conception of virtue. We have seen that as far as the *Republic* is concerned, *elenchus* alone is insufficient. It must be accompanied by a certain kind of nature or disposition, years of musical and athletic training, and a suitable political environment. More important, Plato's description of virtue in the individual makes use of affective ideas like perseverance (442c) or control (443d). In short, virtue involves more than ability to weigh benefit against harm or to admit one's ignorance or to grasp an essential property.

But while Plato has the wherewithall to explain internal conflict, we may question whether the tragic dimension so prevalent in the Socratic dialogues has been eliminated. The *Republic* assumes that a small group of people will turn away from private gain, love of particular people, and devote themselves body and soul to the ascent of knowledge.[28] Once again, we are to believe that they will not want to have things both ways: that as they approach an intuition of the good, they will not be tempted to run away and seek the worship of the crowd. Could we not imagine a person who undergoes the proper training, who recognizes the beauty in what he studies but who, like Alcibiades, resists taking the final step? If we can, then we are right back to the harsh dilemma of the *Symposium*.

Did Plato recognize this? According to Dodds, there is a drift in Plato's philosophy from the "radiant picture of the soul's divine nature and destiny" in the middle dialogues to the pessimism, even despair, of the *Laws*.[29] Whether this is an accurate picture of the development of Plato's thought so that here, too, the tragic dimension prevails, is the subject of another book.

The conclusion of this book is that the Socratic method is neither subject, nor agent, nor situation neutral: it requires a dialogical encounter in which the moral worth of the participants is at stake. To the degree that this encounter is the paradigm for understanding thought in general, discovery, intellectual advancement, always has a practical dimension. If Socrates is right, there is no special branch of learning devoted to moral education. All education worthy of the name imposes moral tests—even mathematics. Once we lose sight of the practical dimension, and learning becomes an impersonal march, the questioner assumes the role of teacher, and the respondent that of student. When this happens, the student can no longer take credit for what is learned and look upon it as his own. Socrates expresses profound skepticism on whether this sort of teaching is possible, whether its successes are really illusory.

The objection to Socrates is that there are obvious reasons for doubting the success of his alternative. Quite apart from discovering the essence of specific virtues, he was unable to persuade many of his respondents of the value of trying. We can defend Socrates and reply to the whole issue of tragedy by saying that he put before us an ideal of inquiry whose ultimate success may be beyond human capabilities. In this respect, it is more a model by which to measure human achievement than a series of steps leading to predictable results. The price we pay for idealizing the Socratic method is that Socrates becomes as much a prophet as a philosopher. He not only points out the inconsistencies in other people's opinions but provides a glimpse of something new, something his contemporaries either could not imagine or imagined but resisted: a life dedicated completely to the pursuit of truth. The Socrates of the *Apology* may have been comfortable with the label of prophet. The problem is that if the label applies, we have no ready-made categories by which to interpret him. He is not an analytic philosopher, a phenomenologist, a pragmatist, or an existentialist. He is a unique person embarked on a mission which he invented. This makes the interpreter's job extraordinarily difficult; but it makes Socrates eternally interesting.

Notes to Chapter Seven

1. *Gorgias*, 418b–c.
2. In addition to *Sophist* 230a, see *Gorgias* 488a and *Republic* 412e–413d. Note that according to *Gorgias* 488a, it is Callicles, not Socrates, who practises admonition.

3. *Nicomachean Ethics* 1145b25–30.
4. Nietzsche, *The Will to Power,* 431.
5. I am here following the interpretation of Gerasimos Santas, "The Socratic Paradoxes," *The Philosophical Review* 73 (1964), 147–164, especially n. 10. With a few exceptions, which Santas points out, this is the most economical reading of the passage. Santas' interpretation is stronger for *Meno* 77e–78b, where nothing in the immediate context suggests Socrates has anything but a prudential sense of "good" and "evil" in mind. For further discussion, see C. C. W. Taylor, *Plato: Protagoras* (Oxford: Clarendon Press, 1967), 165–6. On the other hand, it can be questioned whether the moral and prudential senses of "good" are as distinct as Santas argues. Although the moral and prudential sense of "good" obviously do not *mean* the same thing, it may still be true that they are related by implication. Could a person know that an action is just without knowing that the action will benefit her? I suggest the answer is no. In Chapter Two, I argued against Santas that to know that an action is just, one has to know what justice is. I do not see how *Republic* 443, which refers to vulgar standards of justice, refutes this. If a person knew what justice is, would she not see that justice is beneficial? Contrast: I know what health is in the body but I am unable to decide whether it is beneficial to the body to be healthy. If this situation is impossible, and if the analogy between health and justice is valid, I do not see how a person could know what justice is without knowing that it pays to be just. On the other hand, my argument involves considerations which take one far beyond *Protagoras* 358 or *Meno* 77–78 so that in the interest of economy, I have adopted the prudential reading.
6. Here, too, I am following the lead of Santas, *idid.*
7. On the subject of "irrational" desires, see Irwin, *Plato's Moral Theory, op. cit.,* 78–82. But I do not see any passage in the *Gorgias* or *Lysis* where we are required to assume that it is the *strongest* desire that is focused on the final good as opposed to all desire.
8. *Gorgias* 467c.
9. Cornford, *Cambridge Ancient History,* Vol. VI, 306. Cornford is supported by A.Croiset and L. Bodin, *Platon: Ouevres Complètes* (Paris: Budé 1948), Vol. III, 245, John Gould. *The Development of Plato's Ethics* (Cambridge: Cambridge University Press, 1955), chapter 3, and Gerasimos Santas, "The Socratic Paradoxes," *op. cit.,* 152, n. 15. The overall direction of Cornford's interpretation is challenged by Irwin in *Plato: Gorgias, op. cit.,* 141–2. Irwin's point is that *Gorgias* 467c–d does not imply a distinction between what a person thinks he wants and what he really wants. But while this passage does not imply it alone, it does when read in conjunction with 468d, where the distinction between appearance and reality is clearly drawn. Irwin, *op. cit.,* 145, tries to avoid this conclusion by arguing that the issue is not whether the agent does what he wishes but the

description under which he wishes it. According to Irwin, then, if the tyrant kills someone, there is a sense in which he does what he wishes— namely if we consider the action under a description the agent believed true of it. But where is the evidence that Socrates is willing to use *wish* this way? Irwin's position is perhaps closer to the one articulated by Aristotle at *Nicomachean Ethics* 1113a 21, though even here, *in the strict sense*, wish is directed to true rather than the apparent good.

10. As an etymological matter, wish (*boulēsis*) is a near synonym of desire (*epithumia*), though in some contexts, desire may have wider application. In the *Cratylus* (420a–c), both involve longing for an object, but unlike desire, wish also involves intelligence or reflection. Still, the words are so close in meaning that not everyone could be expected to see the difference. In the *Protagoras* (340b), Socrates attributes the distinction to Prodicus, but Prodicus was known for splitting hairs. In the *Gorgias* (467a ff.), when Socrates draws the contrast between what a person wishes and what seems best to him, Polus' first response is to say that it is "shocking and outrageous." There are, in addition, passages where Socrates appears to use the two words interchangeably, e.g., *Meno* 78a–b, *Symposium* 205a. Cf. *Lysis* 207e and *Republic* 445b.

11. For a discusson of the role of dissatisfaction in the ascent p-assage of the *Symposium*, see J. M. E. Moravcsik, "Reason and *Eros* in the Ascent Passage of the *Sumposium*" in Anton and Kustas (eds.), *Essays in Ancient Greek Philosophy (Albany: SUNY Press, 1972)*, 285–302.

12. Compare Alcibiades' description of Socrates' words to Socrates' own description *at Crito* 54d.

13. Nussbaum, "The Speech of Alcibiades: A Reading of Plato's *Symposium*," *Philosophy and Literature* 3 (1979), 157.

14. Sometimes Socrates talks about examining people's opinions and sometimes (e.g., *Apology* 39c and *Laches* 187e–188a) about examining their lives.The fact is that he is examining the opinions on which their lives are based.

15. See, for example, Sextus Empiricus, *Against the Logicians*, 1.8, 1.190, 1. 264.

16. See, for example, *Laches* 201a–b, *Protagoras* 360e–361d, *Meno* 100a–b.

17. Socrates's respondents often voice a similar complaint. Callicles thinks Socrates has bound and gagged his respondent (*Gorgias* 482e), while Meno thinks he has been drugged (*Meno* 80a–b).

18. The notion that a person is what her knowledge makes her is expressed at *Gorgias* 460b, cf. *Charmides* 169d–e. Although Gorgias accepts the principle, he obviously is not thinking about Socratic *elenchus* when he does.

19. *Protagoras* 352b–c, 358d.

20. The qualification "knowing *or* thinking" is made at *Protagoras* 358c–d. Earlier Socrates had spoken only about knowledge. At *Gorgias* 468, Socrates also uses the neutral "think" instead of "know."

21. See, however, Dostoevsky's *Notes from Underground*, R. E. Matlaw trans. (New York: Dutton, 1960), 7: " . . . I reached the point of feeling a sort of secret abnormal, despicable enjoyment in returning home to my corner on some disgusting Petersburg night, and being acutely conscious that that day I had again done something loathsome, that what was done could never be undone, and secretly, inwardly gnaw at myself for it, nagging and consuming myself till at last the bitterness turned into a sort of shameful accursed sweetness, and finally into real positive enjoyment! Yes, into enjoyment, into enjoyment! I insist upon that. And that is why I have started to speak, because I keep wanting to know for a fact whether other people feel such an enjoyment . . . " But the underground man's position may not be as paradoxical as it sounds. All he has done is make personal freedom the final end. It is possible for Socrates to claim that the underground man suffers from a serious misunderstanding. If so, then like the tyrant and contrary to his own proclamations, he would *not* be doing what he wishes.

22. This raises the question of whether a person with right opinion necessarily has less conviction than a person with knowledge. In view of *Meno* 98b and *Gorgias* 509a, I believe Socrates could argue that *some* right opinion carries with it strong conviction. It appears, however, that the late Academy took a different view, see *Definitions* 414b. Aristotle criticizes the view of the late Academy at *Nicomachean Ethics* 1145b30–1146a5.

23. There is no need to enter the much debated question of whether Plato was adopting hedonism. I side with those who think he was not; he presents it only because it allows him to examine the view of the many. But to say that it is not in human nature to choose a lesser good when one could have a greater is logically independent of saying that pleasure is the greatest good.

24. *Medea* 1075–80 is often taken as a theatrical reply to Socrates. For further discussion, see James J. Walsh, *Aristotle's Conception of Moral Weakness* (New York: Columbia University Press, 1964), Chapter 1.

25. Schimd, "Socratic Moderation and Self-Knowledge," *op. cit.*, 347.

26. It may be significant that Alcibiades' words parallel Socrates' description of right opinion at *Meno* 97e–98a.

27. Nussbaum, *op. cit.*, 167–9.

28. See, for example, *Republic* 486a.

29. Dodds, *The Greeks and the Irrational* (Berkeley and Los Angeles: University of California Press, 1964), Chapter VII.

Appendix
Gorgias' *Apology of Palamedes*[1]

(1) The prosecution and defense do not pass judgment on death for nature herself openly casts a vote against each of us and condemns us to death on the day of our birth. The risk concerns honor and dishonor: whether I must die justly, or violently, under the weight of the greatest censure and the most shameful accusation.

(2) Of the two possibilities, one is entirely in your hands, the other in mine: justice is my decision, violence yours. You easily will be able to kill me, if you wish, for you have power over these matters, while it happens that I have none.

(3) If, then, the accusor, Odysseus, made the accusation out of good will to Greece, either knowing full well that I betrayed Greece to the Barbarians, or in some way believing that I did, he would be among the best of men. For how could this [not] be true of one who rescues his homeland, parents, and all of Greece, while punishing a criminal in the process? But if he has brought the accusation out of jealousy, or craftiness, or wickedness, then just as he was among the noblest of men one the former supposition, he would be among the worst on this one.

(4) Where should I begin in discussing these matters? And what should I say first? To what spot in my defense should I turn? For an unproven accusation produces obvious bewilderment, and because of this bewildermen, I am at a loss to know what to say unless I learn something from the truth itself and from the present, desperate situation, teachers more dangerous than resourceful.

(5) One thing I am clear on is that my accuser accuses me without [knowing] anything clearly. For my own part, I am plainly satisfied that I have done no such thing, nor do I see how someone could know what never happened. But if he made the accusation believing these charges, then as I will prove to you in two ways, he did not speak the truth. For I could not wish to attempt such deeds, if I had the power, nor could I have the power, if I wished.

(6) First, I will take up this argument: that I did not have the power to commit this crime. Now there must have been some first beginning to the act of betrayal, and it would have been in speech, since there must be communica-

155

tion before actions can be undertaken. But how could there be discussions if there had not been some sort of meeting? And how could there have been a meeting unless the other party sent for me or [someone] went from me to him? For not even a written message can arrive without someone to carry it.

(7) Now this can be accomplished with a conversation. Accordingly, if I were together with him, and he associates with me, how did it happen? Who is with whom? Greek with Barbarian. How do we listen or talk to each other? Just by ourselves? But we do not know each other's language. With an interpreter? But then a third party becomes a witness to things which had to be kept secret.

(8) But even if this, too, had happened (which it did not), it was necessary afterwards to give and receive assurances. What would the assurance have been? An oath? Seeing that I was a traitor, who was going to trust me? Were there hostages? Who? Perhaps I would have given my brother (for I had no one else), and the Barbarian, one of his sons. Then there would have been the strongest assurance both from him to me, and from me to him. But if these things happened, they would have been clear to all of you.

(9) Someone will say that we made the pact by exchanging money, the other party giving it, I taking it. Was it for a small amount? But it is not likely that someone would take a small amount of money in exchange for a large undertaking. Was it for a large amount? Then who delivered it? How could [one] person have done so? Were many people involved? But many people delivering the money would have meant many witnesses to the plot. Yet, if there was one person, he could not have been carrying anything very valuable.

(10) Was it delivered during the day or night? But there are many closely stationed guards whose attention could not be avoided. During the day time? But the light would make this impossible. Very well. Did I go out to receive it or did the other party bring it here? Both are impractical. If I did, in fact, take it, how would I have concealed it from those both inside and outside the camp? Where would I have put it? How would I have protected it? If I used it, I would have exposed myself. If I did not use it, what good would I have derived from it?

(11) Yet, even though this did not happen, assume that it did. We got together, talked, listened, I took the money from them, took it in secret, and hid it. It then was necessary, I presume, to do the action for the sake of which all of this occurred. Yet this is even more impractical than the things I just mentioned. In doing it, I acted alone or with others. But this was not the activity of one person. Were there others? Who? Obviously associates. Were they free or slave? But you are the free men with whom I associate. Which of you, then, was privy to my action? Let him speak. And how is it possible that I acted with slaves? For they make accusations both voluntarily, desiring to gain their freedom, and when tortured, out of sheer necessity.

(12) How, in fact, [would] the action have occurred? Clearly it was necessary to have enemy troops stronger than you enter the camp, which is impossible. How, then, would I have gotten them in? Through the gates? But I did not have the authority either to open or shut them. The commanders are in charge. Over the walls with a ladder? Wouldn't [I have been spotted?] For the entire area was full of guards. Through a wall then? This would have been obvious to everyone. This being a military camp, life takes place around weapons in an open environment in which [everyone] sees everything, and everyone is seen by everyone else. So taking everything into account, it was utterly impossible for me to do any of these things.

(13) Let us consider together the following point as well. Supposing I was eminently capable of these things, what was my motive in wishing to do them? After all, no one wishes to risk the greatest dangers for nothing nor even to be utterly wicked by accomplishing the foulest of deeds. What, then, was my motive? [Once again, I return to this point.] Was it to rule? Over you or the Barbarians? But it would be impossible for me to rule over you in view of your number, your nature, and the fact that you are endowed with every type of valuable resource: noble ancestors, a full measure of wealth, excellence of character, strong resolution, and the kingship of cities.

(14) Over the [Barbarians] then? Which of them is about to surrender? By what sort of power will I, a Greek, gain ascendency over Barbarians; I being one, they being many? Persuasion or violence? But they would not wish to be persuaded and neither would I have the power to use force against them. But perhaps there are some who are willing to betray them to an equally willing enemy by receiving money in payment for their treachery. But to accept this and believe it is the height of folly. For who prefer slavery to kingship, the worst state of affairs to the best?

(15) Someone could say that I attempted these things out of love of wealth and money. But I have an adequate amount of money and have no need for large sums. Those who spend a great deal of money need a great deal, but not those who are master of the natural pleasures; rather, it is those who are slaves to pleaure and seek to acquire honors from wealth and pretension. None of this applies to me. As reliable evidence for the truth of what I am saying, I will offer my previous life. Surely you can bear witness to this testimony for you are my comrades and therefore know these things.

(16) Nor would a person with a reasonable amount of discretion attempt to do these things for the sake of honor. For honors result from excellence, not from wickedness. How would honor come to one who was a traitor to Greece? Besides, it happens that honor is something I do not lack for I am honored for the most honorable of things by the most honorable of men—by you for wisdom.

(17) Neither would a person do these things for the sake of security. The traitor is the enemy of everything: the law, justice, the gods, and the rest of

mankind for he violates the law, does away with justice, ruins the rest of mankind, and disgraces the holy. [A] life of this sort which involves the greatest dangers does not contain security.

(18) Did I wish to help friends or harm enemies? For someone could commit a crime for these motives. Yet in my case, exactly the opposite was true: I harmed my friends and aided my enemies. Thus the action in no way led to the acquisition of good things, and no one lays the villain out of a desire to suffer harm.

(19) It remains to consider whether I did this to avoid some fear or distress or danger. But no one could say that these factors applied to me. All actions which people perform are done for two reasons: either to pursue some advantage or avoid some loss. Whatever treacherous actions are committed for reasons other than these [customarily land the person who does them in terrible evils. That I would have] harmed myself [most of all] by doing these things is not hard to see.[2] In betraying Greece, I was betraying myself, my parents, friends, the reputation of my ancestors, the religion of my native country, sacred burial places, and my great native country itself: Greece. Those things which are of supreme importance to every person I would have entrusted to criminals.[3]

(20) Consider the following as well. Wouldn't my life have been unlivable if I had done these things? Where was I to turn for solace? To Greece? Am I going to make amends with those who have been wronged? Who among those who suffered could keep away from me? Will I remain with the Barbarians? Will I disregard everything of importance, robbed of the highest honor, living out my life in utter disgrace, renouncing the work done for the sake of excellence in earlier days? And this a result of my own doing, when to bring misfortune on oneself is the most shameful thing of all.

(21) What is more, I would not even be trusted among the Barbarians. For how could anyone trust me knowing lthat I had done the most untrustworthy of deeds: betraying friends to enemies? Yet life is not worth living for someone who has been stripped of respect. For the person who loses his money [or] falls from power or is exiled from his native land might recovery, but the person who throws away respect could not get it back again. Thus is has been proved by what has been said that I could not wish to betray Greece [if I had the power, nor could I have the power, if I wished.]

(22) Following these remarks, I would like to address the accuser. In what do you trust when, being the sort of person you are, you accuse someone like me? It is worth examining what kind of person it takes to say the things you do: an unworthy man accusing someone unworthy of the charge. Do you accuse me knowing exactly what happened or merely believing it? For it you know, your knowledge results from seeing what happened, taking part in it, or learning [from someone who took part]. If, therefore, you saw, describe for these peole [the manner], the place, the time, when, where, how you saw it. If, however, you took part, you are liable on the same charges. Finally, if you

heard from someone who took part, who is he? Let him come forward, present himself, and give testimony. Since neither of us is offering witnesses, the accusation will be more believable if proven in this way.

(23) Perhaps you will say that it is fair for you not to offer witnesses in support of your version of what happened, but that I should offer them in support of my version of what did not. Yet this is not fair because it is utterly impossible to have testified about what never occurred. But in regard to what did occur, not only is it not impossible, it is quite easy, and not only easy, [but necessary. Yet] in your case, it was not so, [and not] only did you find witnesses, you did not even find false ones. In my case, however, it was possible to find neither.

(24) It is clear, then, that you do not have knowledge of the facts upon which you brought the accusation. Since you do [not] have knowledge, the remaining possibility is that you have opinion. Accordingly, do you, most daring of men, trusting in opinion, a wholly untrustworthy source, not knowing the truth, dare to ask for the death penalty? Why are you privy to the knowledge that such a thing was done? It is perfectly natural for everyone to have opinions on every subject, and in this respect, you are no wiser than anyone else. Yet neither is it right to trust in opinions rather than knowledge nor to recognize opinion as being more trustworthy than truth. Rather, the opposite is the case: truth is more trustworthy than opinion.

(25) You accused me on the basis of claims originating from two contradictory sources: wisdom and madness, things which cannot belong to the same person. Where you assert that I am adept as well as both clever and resourceful, you accuse me of wisdom; where you assert that I betrayed Greece, you accuse me of madness. It is, after all, madness to embark on exploits which are impossible, inexpedient, disgraceful, harmful to one's friends, advantageous to his enemies, and bound to make one's own life shameful and dangerous. How can one believe someone like this, who in the same breath says to the same people the most contradictory things about the same subject?

(26) I would like to learn from you whether you regard intelligent people as foolish or thoughtful. If foolish, then your speech is novel but not true; if thoughtful, then I presume it is unfitting for thoughtful people to commit the most grievous errors and the prefer evils to present goods. If, therefore, I am wise, I have not gone wrong; if I have gone wrong, I am not wise. In both cases, you would be mistaken.

(27) I do not wish to make counter-charges dealing with the many grave offenses you have committed, both old and new, but I could. For [it is my wish] to escape this charge not be recounting your vices but by recounting my virtues. Hence this is all I have to say to you.

(28) To you, my judges, I wish to say something about myself which is injurious though true—not suitable for one who has [not] been accusedf, but) perfectly fitting for one who has. For I am now undergoing scrutiny at your

hands and giving an account of my past. Therefore, if I recall some of the noble things I have done, I ask you not to take offense at what is said, but to realize that it is necessary for one cleverly and falsely accused to say, in addition, some genuinely good things to those of you who know them. This is the most pleasant thing for me.

(29) First, then, and second, and most important of all, in every respect, from beginning to end, my past life has been faultless, completely free of guilt. No one could speak to you truthfully and ascribe any responsibility for evil to me. In fact, not even the accuser himself has offered any proof for what he has said. Thus his speech has the force of mere abuse without proof.

(30) I would say, and in saying it would not be speaking falsely nor be open to refutation, that not only am I innocent, I am a great benefactor to you, and the Greeks, and all men—not just to those living now but to those to come [as well]. For who would have taken human life from scarcity to plenitude and from barrenness to finery by inventing military tactics of the greatest advantage, [and] written laws, the guardians of justice, and letters, the instrument of memory, and both weights and measures which facilitate commercial exchange, and number, the guardian of property, both the most powerful beacons and the swiftest messengers, and draughts, an enjoyable way of spending leisure time? What then, is my reason for reminding you of these things?

(31) It is to make clear [on the one hand] that it is to things like these that I devote my attention, and to offer proof that I abstain from shameful and wicked deeds, on the other. For it is impossible for a person devoting his attention to the latter also to pay attention to things like the former. Moreover, it is fitting that I myself should not suffer harm at your hands if you have not suffered at mine.

(32) And neither is it fair for me to be harmed on account of other pursuits, whether by the young or the old. For I am inoffensive to the older, yet not useless to the younger, not jealous of the fortunate, merciful to the unfortunate, neither contemptuous of poverty nor prizing wealth more than virtue, but virtue more than wealth; neither useless in council nor idle in battle, carrying out orders, obeying the leaders. Now it is not for me to praise myself; however, having been accused of these things, the present occasion forces me to mount a defense in every way I can.

(33) The remainder of my speech concerns you and is directed to you. When I am finished with it, I will end my defense. Appeals to pity, entreaties, the supplications of friends are helpful when the trial takes place before a crowd; but when it is before you, first among the Greeks and men of good repute, it is not proper to persuade you by using the help of friends, nor entreaties, nor pity. Rather, it is proper for me to escape this charge by appealing to the clearest principles of justice, putting forth the truth, and not entangling in deception.

(34) You must not pay more attention to words than you do to actions, neither should you prejudge the grounds for my defense, think that a short time will result in a wiser decision than a long one, nor regard slander as more

cedible than first hand experience. For good men always exercise great care to avoid doing wrong, and all the more so in those matters which cannot be corrected than in those which can. For such things are under the control of those who exercised foresight, and cannot be corrected by those with hindsight. A matter of this sort arises whenever people judge someone on capital charges, which is the situation in which you now find yourselves.

(35) If, then, words could both reveal the truth about actions and put it in view of the listeners, based on what has been said, the decision would be easy. However, since thise is not the case, protect me, wait a while longer, and decide the case on the side of truth. For there is a great danger that by appearing unjust, you will lose one reputation only to gain another. To good men, death is preferable to a disgraceful reputation: one is the end of life, the other a sickness which infects it.

(36) If you do, in fact, kill me unjustly, it will be evident to many people for I am [not] unknown, and your wickedness will come to light so that all Greeks may learn of it. Moreover, it will be manifest to everyone that the responsibility for injustice lies with you, not with the accuser. For the outcome of the trial is in your hands. A more serious mistake than this could not be made. For it you reach an unjust verdict, not only will you have made a mistake in regard to me and my parents, but your actions will bring you collective responsibility for a terrible, unholy, unjust, and unlawful deed, having put to death a man who is your comrade, useful to you, and a benefactor to Greece. It would amount to Greek killing Greek, when it has not been shown that he committed any discernible crime or is guilty of any credible charge.

(37) My side of the case has been given, and I rest. It makes sense to provide bad judges with a brief reminder of what has been said, but it is not worthy of the reputation of the very first among Greeks to think that they neither pay attention to or remember what has been said.

Notes to Appendix

1. The text is that of Diels and Krantz, *Die Fragments Der Vorsokratiker*, 16th ed., Vol. II, 82. B. 11a. All interpolations are put in brackers, and unless otherwise noted, follow the suggestions of Diels.

   I have consulted the translation of George Kennedy in Rosamond Kent Sprague (ed.) *The Older Sophists* (Columbia, South Carolina: Univ. of South Carolina Press, 1972), 54–63. Where Kennedy strives for a literal rendering of the Greek, I aim for a version which sounds more like a speech.

2. There is a gap in the text at this point, and the material in brackets is an interpolation of Keil. Since this suggestion is accepted by Diels, I have included it in translation. For my part, however, Lucke's suggestion (i.e.

that treacherous actions done for reasons other than seeking advantage or avoiding loss are mad) is probably closer to the original sense.

3. The text reads: "to men who were wronged." However, Diels is certainly correct in speculating that "men who did wrong" is the true sense.

Bibliography

Adam, J., *Plato's Euthyphro* (Cambridge: Cambridge University Press, 1908).

Adkins, A. H. *Merit and Responsibility* (Oxford: Clarendon Press, 1960).

Allen, R. E., ed., *Studies in Plato's Metaphysics* (New York: Humanities Press, 1965).

———, *Plato's "Euthyphro" and the Earlier Theory of Forms* (New York: Humanities Press, 1970).

———, *Socrates and Legal Obligation* (Minneapolis: University of Minnesota Press, 1980).

Annas, J., ed. *Oxford Studies in Ancient Philosophy* (Oxford: Clarendon Press, 1983).

Anton, J. P. and Kustas, G. L., eds. *Essays in Ancient Greek Philosophy*, Vol. 1, (Albany: SUNY Press, 1971).

———, and Preus, A., *Essays in Ancient Greek Philosophy*, Vol. II (Albany: SUNY Press, 1983).

Beckman, J., *The Religious Dimension of Socrates' Thought* (Waterloo, Ontario: Canadian Corporation for Studies in Religion, 1979).

Bluck, R. S., *Plato's Phaedo* (London: Routledge & Kegan Paul, 1955).

———, *Plato's Meno* (Cambridge: Cambridge University Press, 1964).

Brague, R., *Le Restant: Supplément aux Commentaires du Ménon de Platon* (Paris: Vrin, 1978).

Brickhouse, T. C., and Smith, N. D., "The Origin of Socrages' Mission," *The Journal of the History of Ideas*, 44 (1983), 657–666.

Brown, M., "Plato Disapproves of the Slave-Boy's Answer," *Review of Metaphysics* 20 (1967), 57–93.

163

Brumbaugh, R. S., *Plato's Mathematical Imagination* (New Haven: Yale University Press, 1954).

———, "Plato's *Meno* as Form and Content of Secondary School Courses in Philosophy," *Teaching Philosophy* 1-2 (1975), 107–115.

✗ Brun, J., *Socrates*, translated by D. Scott (New York: Walker and Co., 1962).

Burnet, J., *Plato's Phaedo* (Oxford: Clarendon Press, 1911).

———, *Plato's Euthyphro, Apology of Socrates, and Crito* (Oxford: Clarendon Press, 1924).

Burnyeat, M. F., "Virtues in Action," in Vlastos (ed.), *The Philosophy of Socrates*, 209–234.

———, "Socratic Midwifery, Platonic Inspiration," *Bulletin of the Institute of Classical Studies* 24 (1977), 7–13.

———, "Examples in Epistemology: Socrates, Theaetetus, and G. E. Moore," *Philosophy* 52 (1977), 381–398.

Bury, R. G., *The Symposium of Plato*, second edition (Cambridge: Cambridge University Press, 1932).

Calogero, G., "Gorgias and the Socratic Principle: *Nemo Sua Sponte Peccat*," *Journal of Hellenic Studies* 77 (1957), 12-7.

Cherniss, H. F., "The Philosophical Economy of the Theory of Ideas," *American Journal of Philosophy* 57 (1936), 445–456.

———, *Aristotle's Criticism of Plato and the Academy* (Baltimore: The Johns Hopkins Press, 1944).

———, *The Riddle of the Early Academy* (Berkeley: University of California Press, 1945).

———, "Plato as Mathematician," *Review of Metaphysics* 4(1951), 395–425.

✗ Chroust, A. H., *Socrates: Man and Myth* (London: Routledge & Kegan Paul, 1957).

Cornford, F. M., "Mathematics and Dialectic in the *Republic* VI-VII," in Allen (ed.), *Studies in Plato's Metaphysics*, 61–95.

———, *Plato's Theory of Knowledge* (London: Routledge & Kegan Paul, 1935).

———, *The Unwritten Philosophy* (Cambridge: Cambridge University Press, 1950).

———, *Principium Sapientiae* (Cambridge: Cambridge University Pres, 1952).

Coulter, J. A., "The Relation of the *Apology of Socrates* to Gorgias' *Defense of Palamedes* and Plato's Critique of Gorgianic Rhetoric," *Harvard Studies in Classical Philosophy* 68 (1964), 269–303.

Croiset, A. and Bodin, L., *Platon: Ouevres Complètes*, Vol. III (Paris: Budé, 1949).

Devereux, D., "Nature and Teaching in Plato's *Meno*," *Phronesis* 23 (1978), 118–26.

Dilman, I., *Morality and the Inner Life: A Study in Plato's Gorgias* (London: Macmillan, 1979).

Dodds, E. R., *The Greeks and the Irrational* (Berkeley and Los Angeles: University of California Press, 1951).

———, *Plato Gorgias* (Oxford: Clarendon Press, 1959).

Dover, J. K., *Greek Popular Morality in the Time of Plato and Aristotle* (Oxford: Blackwell, 1974).

Elias, J. A., *Plato's Defense of Poetry* (Albany: SUNY Press, 1984).

Findlay, J. N., *Plato: The Written and Unwritten Doctrines* (London: Routledge and Kegan Paul, 1974).

Findley, M. I., *Aspects of Antiquity* (New York: Viking, 1960).

Freeman, K., *Compansion to the Pre-Socratic Philosophers* (Oxford: Blackwell, 1952).

Frege, G., *The Foundations of Arithmetic*, translated by J. L. Austin (Oxford: Clarendon Press, 1959).

Friedländer, P., *Plato: An Introduction*, translated by H. Meyerhoff (New York: Bollingen Foundation, 1958).

———, *Plato: The Dialogues, First Period*, translated by H. Meyerhoff (New York: Bollingen, 1964).

———, *Plato: The Dialogues, Second and Third Periods*, translated by H. Meyerhoff (Princeton: Bollingen, 1969).

Frutiger, P., *Les Mythes de Platon* (Paris: Alcan, 1930).

Gallop, D., *Plato Phaedo* (Oxford: Clarendon Press, 1975).

Geach, P. T., "Plato's *Euthyphro*: An Analysis and Commentary," *The Monist* 50 (1966), 369–382.

Gomperz, H., *Sophistik und Rhetorik* (Leipzig: Teubner, 1912).

Gould, J., *The Development of Plato's Ethics* (Cambridge: Cambridge University Press, 1955?.

Gould, Josiah, :"Klein on Ethological Mimes, for example, that *Meno, Journal of Philosophy* 66 (1969), 253–65.

Grote, G., *Plato, and the Other Companions of Socrates*, Vol.'s I and II, third edition (London: John Murray, 1875).

Gulley, N., *Plato's Theory of Knowledge* (London: Methuen, 1962).

——, *The Philosophy of Socrates* (London: Macmillan, 1968).

Guthrie, W. K. C., *The Greeks and Their Gods* (Boston: Beacon Press, 1950).

——, *A History of Greek Philosophy*, Vol. III (Cambridge: Cambridge University Press, 1969).

Hackforth, R. M., *The Composition of Plato's Apology* (Cambridge: Cambridge University Press, 1933).

——, *Plato's Phaedrus* (Cambridge: Cambridge University Press, 1952).

Hansing, O., "Plato's Doctrine of Recollection," *The Monist* 38 (1928), 261–2.

Hathaway, R., "Explaining the Unity of the Platonic Dialogue," *Philosophy and Literature* 8 (1984). 195–208.

Hyland, D., "Why Plato Wrote Dialogues," *Philosophy and Rhetoric* (1968), 38–50.

Irwin, T., *Plato's Moral Theory* (Oxford: Clarendon Press, 1977).

——, *Plato Gorgias* (Oxford: Clarendon Press, 1979).

Jaeger, W., *The Theory of the Early Greek Philosophers* (Oxford: Clarendon Press, 1947).

Kant, I., *Groundwork of the Metaphysics of Morals*, Paton trans. (New York: Harper and Row, 1948)

Kierkegaard, S., *Philosophical Fragments*, revised translation by H. V. Hong Princeton: Princeton University Press, 1962).

Klein, J., *A Commentary on Plato's Meno* (Chapel Hill: University of North Carolina Press, 1965).

Knox, B., *Oedipus at Thebes* (New Haven: Yale University Press, 1957; rpt. New York: Norton, 1972).

Koyré, M., *Discovering Plato*, translated by L. C. Rosenfield (New York: Columbia University Press, 1945).

Kraut, R., *Socrates and the State* (Princeton: Princeton University Press, 1984).

⅄ Lacey, A. R., "Our Knowledge of Socrates," in Vlastos (ed.), *The Philosophy of Socrates*, 22-49.

Merlan, P., "Form and Content in Plato's Philosophy," *Journal of the History of Philosophy* (1947), 406-30.

Morgan, M., "How Does Plato Solve the Paradox of Inquiry in the *Meno*?" unpublished manuscript presented to the Society of Ancient Greek Philosophy, Chicago, 1985.

Moravcsik, J. M. E., "Learning as Recollection," in Vlastos (ed.), *Plato* Vol. I, 53-69.

———, "Reason and Eros in the 'Ascent' passage of the *Symposium*," in Anton and Kustas (ed.), *Essays in Greek Philosophy*, 285-302.

Morrow, G., *Plato's Epistles* (Indianapolis: Bobbs-Merrill, 1962).

Nadler, S., "Probability and Truth in The *Apology*," *Philosophy and Literature* 9 (1985), 198-201.

Nettleship, R. L., *Lectures on Plato's Republic*, second edition (1901; rpt. New York: St. Martins Press, 1967).

Nietzsche, F., *The Will to Power*, translated by W. Kaufman and Hollingdale (New York: Random House, 1967).

———, *The Birth of Tragedy*, translated by W. Kaufman (New York: Random House, 1976).

Nilsson, M. P., *Greek Piety*, translated by H. J. Rose (New York: Norton, 1969).

Nussbaum, M., "The Speech of Alcibiades: A Reading of Plato's *Symposium*," *Philosophy and Literature* 3 (1979), 131-2.

O'Brien, M. J., "The Unity of the *Laches*," in Anton and Kustas (eds.), *Essays in Ancient Greek Philosophy*, 303-15.

Owen, G. E. L., (ed.), *Aristotle on Dialectic*. (London: Oxford University Press, 1968).

Owens, J., *An Elementary Christian Metaphysics* (Milwaukee: Bruce Publishing Co., 1968).

Penner, T., "The Unity of Virtue," *Philosophical Review* 82 (1973) 35-68.

Phillipson, C., *The Trial of Socrates* (London: Stevens, 1926).

Popper, K., *The Logic of Scientific Discovery* (London: Hutchinson, 1959).

Rabinowitz, W. G., "Platonic Piety: An Essay Toward the Solution of an Enigma," *Phronesis* 3 (1958), 108-120.

Randall, J. H., *Dramatist of the Life of Reason* (New York: Columbia University Press, 1977).

Rawls, J., *A Theory of Justice* (Cambridge: Harvard University Press, 1971).

Robinson, R., "Analysis in Greek Geometry," *Mind* n.s. 45 (1936), 464-73.

———, *Plato's Earlier Dialectic*, second edition (London: Oxford University Press, 1953).

Romilly, J., *Magic and Rhetoric in Ancient Greece* (Cambridge: Harvard University Press, 1975).

Rorty, F., *Philosophy and the Mirror of Nature* (Princeton: Princeton University Press, 1975).

Santas, G., "The Socratic Paradoxes," *The Philosphical Review* 73 (1964), 147-64.

———, "The Socratic Fallacy," *Journal of the History of Philosophy* 10 (1974).

———, *Socrates: Philosophy in Plato's Early Dialogues* (London: Routledge & Kegan Paul, 1979).

Sayre, K., *Plato's Analytic Method* (Chicago: University of Chicago Press, 1969).

Schmid, T., "Socratic Moderation and Self-Knowledge," *Journal of the History of Philosophy*, 21 (1983), 339-348.

Solmsen, F., "Dialectic Without the Forms," in Owen (ed.), *Aristotle on Dialectic*, 49-68.

Sprague, R. K., *The Older Sophists* (Columbia, S.C., University of South Carolina Press, 1972).

Stenzel, J., Plato's Method of Dialectic, translated by D. J. Allan (Oxford: Clarendon Press, 1940).

Stock, St. G., *The Meno of Plato* (Oxford: Clarendon Press, 1887).

Strauss, L., *The City and Man* (Chicago: University of Chicago Press, 1964).

Tarrant, D., "Style and Thought in Plato's Dialogues," *Classical Quarterly* 42 (1948), 28-34.

Tate, J., "Greek for 'Atheism,'" *Classical Review* 50 (1936), 3-5.

———, "More Greek for 'Atheism,'" *Classical Review* 51 (1937), 3-6.

Taylor, C. C. W., *Plato Protagoras* (Oxford: Clarendon Press, 1976).

Teloh, H., *The Development of Plato's Metaphysics* (University Park: The Pennsylvania State University Press, 1981).

Thomas, J. E., *Musings on the Meno* (The Hague: Martinus Nijhoff, 1980).

Thompson, E. E., *The Meno of Plato* (London: MacMillan, 1901).

Tuckey, T. G., *Plato's Charmides* (Cambridge: Cambridge University Press, 1951).

Versényi, L., *Socratic Humanism* (New Haven: Yale University Press, 1968).

Vlastos, G., "Socratic Knowledge and Platonic Pessimism," *Philosophical Review* 66 (1957), 226-38.

———, "*Anamnesis* in the *Meno*," *Dialogue* 4 (1965), 143-67.

———, (ed.) *Plato* Vol. I (Garden City, N.Y.: Doubleday, 1970).

———, (ed.) *The Philosophy of Socrates* (Garden City, N.Y.: Doubleday, 1971).

———, "The Paradox of Socrates," in Vlastos (ed.), *The Philosophy of Socrates*, 1-21.

———, (ed.) *Platonic Studies*, second edition (Princeton: Princeton University Press, 1981).

———, "What did Socrates Understand by His 'What is F?' Question," in Vlastos (ed.), *Platonic Studies*, second edition, 410-17.

———, "The Socratic Elenchus," in Annas (ed.), *Oxford Studies in Ancient Philosophy*, 27-58.

Walsh, J. J., *Aristotle's Conception of Moral Weakness* (New York: Columbia University Press, 1964).

Weingartner, R., *The Unity of the Platonic Dialogue* (Indianapolis: Bobbs-Merrill, 1973).

White, N. P., "Inquiry," *Review of Metaphysics* 26 (1972), 289-310.

———, *Plato on Knowledge and Reality* (Indianapolis: Hackett, 1976).

The following articles came to my attention too late to be considered:

Desjardins, R., "Knowledge and Virtue: Paradox in Plato's *Meno*," *Review of Metaphysics* 39 (1985), 261-281.

McPherran, M. L., "Socratic Piety in The *Evthyphro*," *Journal of The History of Philosophy* 23 (1985), 283-309.

Index of Names

Index of Subjects

Index of Sources